THE DANCE SCHOOL OWNER'S SURVIVAL GUIDE:

Everything you need to set up and run a successful dance school.

Second edition

Sarah Gittins

ISBN: 978-1-910662-34-2

First published in 2016

Second edition

CONTENTS

Introduction

Dance is the most amazing form of self-expression, both a release and an art form, creative, brilliant, fulfilling and pure enjoyment. If, like me, it's in your blood, you miss it when it's not there, and you love every minute you are dancing. However, there is a dark side – like fashion, dance is notoriously fickle, highly competitive and often cut-throat. But this isn't a book about how to become the next well-known dancer – that's a whole different scenario. This is about owning your own successful and profitable dance school, taking that amazing leap into creating something amazing that is yours, a school that runs to your rules, your ideas and your ideals. It's the most incredible privilege to pass on your knowledge to the younger generation, and that's your passion. But, and this is a big 'but', ultimately you are running a business!

Who am I? And what makes me the person to tell you how to run *your* dance school?

18 years ago, I had a passion – a dream about opening my own dance school. I had assisted for years, studied, got my degree and I loved teaching. So when I was 22, just out of university, the dance school I assisted at offered me the chance to buy the school. Then, I felt the timing wasn't right. I wanted to see the world, gain more experience and push my choreographic and creative boundaries. Amongst other things, I gained a position in Greece choreographing for a five-star hotel company, being flown around, creating shows, choreographing up to 30 routines a week in various situations, locations, abilities and working across 13 languages. On reflection this was an incredible education, I had to continually think on my feet, adapt and be inventive in the craziest situations (I have some stories, trust me!) I became an expert at thinking out of the box, being calm in a crisis and getting creative.

When I returned to the UK, I started working again for other dance and theatre schools, theatres and professional companies. My dream to open my own school became a reality when I came up with a new concept of dance school. At the time, everything in our area was exam-based or specialist. I decided to offer dance classes to those who did not want the traditional dance school – it was for fun, with no exams and no uniform, and very different to what was out there. I was also the first to offer street dance, and this hit just on the up-curve of the street dance trend. The school grew fast. Yet again, I had to adapt fast and learn the rules of business as I went along. I made mistakes along the way, I don't mind admitting that, because ultimately I am human and it's how you learn from those mistakes that matter. But I also made some really good calls. Even now, I manage to stay ahead. You can call it intuition, gut feeling, business acumen, or a blend of all three!

So, for 18 years I have run my own successful multi-venue dance school, with student numbers around 300, even during a recession. The competition in my location is fierce, so survival and growth has meant staying on top of trends, marketing, staying at the top of that dance school market. I have also written, devised and produced my own shows and events. I have pretty much got the t-shirt in every colour (including a few you wouldn't expect!) The wealth of knowledge and experience I can share with you, will ultimately save you thousands of pounds, endless hours of wasted time and will stop you making unnecessary mistakes. If you start your new business on the right foot (excuse the pun!) it lays the groundwork so that your business can work for you. Pretty much like dance – you learn the basics and it provides a stable foundation on which you can grow.

So, this book comes from a place of experience, and it gives an honest approach about what you need to do before opening your own dance school. Or maybe you already have your own dance school, but things are not working right, you feel overwhelmed, or there are things that you are missing and didn't realise you needed – I call this 'getting your house in order'. With a stronger business focus, you can progress and grow your dance school.

Using this book, you can learn from my mistakes and success so you can apply the things that really work to your business. This can lead you to profitability quicker, can help you get more students through the door, create sell-out shows and help guide you away from the problems that will eventually arise. I wish I had this resource 17 years ago. It would have saved me thousands and a lot of hassle!

PREPARATION

Before You Think About Opening

Chapter 1

WHAT TO EXPECT

What to expect

Let's be crystal clear from the outset – opening and running a dance school is opening a business. Whether that turns out to be one or two classes in the local church hall or a multi-venue school, business is business and you are about to start one. Therefore you need to abide by your country's business laws and comply with health and safety, insurance and risk assessment regulations.

Secondly, as creative people, we're passionate about dance and we do it because we want to and we LOVE it! OK, it's great to be passionate and love what you're doing, that's crucial – but, and this is a massive sticking point, you're in business and businesses make money.

If you have no interest in making money, but you still have the passion and drive to open a dance school, then make it a not-for profit or a charity – that way you can still access funding. This book goes into detail on making a profitable dance school.

Even though it's a passion and a love, you can still earn a good living from this. Someone once told me, 'You will never make money in dance.' But why not? Why can't you make money in dance? After all, it's a business and if your profit margins break even and your marketing is right, it offers an opportunity to make a very good living, you just have to step forward and take it.

I'm going to get on my soap box now. Too many dancers are working for nothing, earning their stripes. And this culture appears to filter down to how dance school owners operate. You give everything, and then you have nothing left, and wonder why you are always exhausted and don't have much to show for it.

Stop doing it! Take a breather and start to run a business – not a community drop-in where parents get something for nothing. All your years of training *are* worth something, all your dedication to the technique is worth something; value yourself, your craft and your skill. Your expertise *is* worth money. Respect yourself enough to ask for it. OK, I'm off my soap box now.

People ask me, what's your 9-5 job? I answer 'this is it'. My full-time job is running a dance school, so it has to earn enough money to pay my mortgage, put food on the table and clothes on my kids – no excuses. This is my job, it pays a full-time wage month in, month out, and my dance school only runs 33 weeks a year!

Do you have the skills required to be self-employed?

You will need:

- Technical skills
- Marketing skills
- Financial skills

With that goes a whole bunch of other jobs! Now I am not saying that to scare you off, but let's have eyes open on this, Running your own business involves wearing MANY hats. That is the fun of it as well – you get to have such variety, but it also means you can be a jack of all trades and master of none. Bring it back to dance. Your trade is the skill, the teaching the knowledge of technique; if you are not an expert at finance then BEFORE you open take a course. Do an overview of where you are now and what skills you need and start learning.

I am still learning, 18 years on. I am currently taking a management course. Grab a book, listen to a podcast, start an online course with a site like Open University and Udemy. Also, local government and even local businesses run funded courses that you can jump on and up your 'other'skills.

So you're a Dance School Principal!

You are also a.....

Accountant
Book Keeper
Marketing Manager
Receptionist
CEO
Entrepreneur
Technician
Strategist
IT Specalist
Designer
Events Organiser
Administrator
Producer
Marketing consultant
Cleaner
Business Manager
Health and Safety Executive
Writer
DJ
Stage Manager
Hall Manager
Costume Designer
Seamstress
Social Media Consultant
Prop Maker
Role Model
Set Designer
Human Resource Manager
Legal Department
Fire Safety Officer
Merchandiser
Shop Owner
Teacher
Childminder (feels like at times!)
and a bloody taxi driver!!!!!

So next time someone says - Oh you run a few classes! Tell them to shove it!

www.thedanceden.co.uk

In amongst all those 'other' jobs, I really need to mention mind-set. In 2013, I hit burnout BIG style and suffered a breakdown. Dance took me there. I do not exaggerate when I say I could not have got any lower. Burn out and/or undisclosed mental illness is HUGE in the industry because we are frequently being 'headless chickens' and normality is a firefighting exercise. This HAS to change! Dance in its nature is competitive. It is a constant transition of styles and developments; there's always the next 'in' thing. And then throw into the mix creativity. As creative people by nature we are passionate, and often that passion can blind us or tunnel vision us down a path where we forget our needs.

Don't get me wrong, when you have shows, competitions or exam times then you are always going to be busy. But I stress... this should be for short periods of time. If you are continually firefighting then this is NOT good on you.

There are going to be times when you doubt yourself, or second guess why you are doing this, or have a parent upset you by snapping at you. I would love to say this book will stop all of that, but only YOU can control your mind. What I'm saying is, don't go into this blind. In this book I'll keep coming back to and this will really help; but your mind is *your* responsibility. Keep it strong, keep it healthy, take time for *you* and be selfish about it – and that's ok too. As teachers we give all the time. Remember to take time, rest, and get inspiration for yourself. Build this in from an early stage, and don't be blinkered and naïve enough to think that opening a dance school is going to be all sweetness and light. It won't be – and I am sorry. However, show me any business that does not go through the same! Every business does, so don't sweat it. Every business is run by someone different, therefore the mind-set will always be different, and that bit is up to you. Be sure to take care of you!

Why you should do it

If you are that person who can take the stress and strain of running a business it's the most rewarding, infuriating, inspired, stressful, amazing job in the world. For all my tears, I would not change a single thing from the past 18 years. I love the freedom that having my own business gives me. No asking permission for a dentist trip or explaining to a boss why I need a sofa day with my kids when they're sick. Coffee with the girls on a Friday morning? Yes please! But for all the lovely elements above, I need to add in the 2am finishes, lugging my laptop on holiday, and other such delights. I'm actually writing this book in the car on the way to Scotland! The stress is immense. **A dance school is its own animal and I think that you can't reallt comment until you have run one yourself.**

Do not take opening new businesses lightly. Ask yourself:

Why are you opening? Is it just a few classes? Are you really just coming from a place of passion, or are you truly thinking about it as a business that comes from a place of passion?

Are you ready to work hard?

Are you ready to work on sociable hours?

Are you ready to deal with contracts and legalities?

Are you ready to make mistakes and learn?

Are you ready to do all the things that you need to do?

Is what you are planning to open going to make money?

Because just running a few classes is not how the HMRC see it. You still need to pay taxes as a business. Your few classes still need to be a business.

You have to get your foundations right from the beginning. This needs serious research. Do your homework, because without this then you are going to make more mistakes than you need to. These will either cost you a lot of money, either through making financial mistakes or through heartache, because you don't want to start your school, get a load of students in and then lose them because you have not got your foundations right.

So are you ready to make the leap? Olympic runners don't start a race thinking 'I'll just have a little run and a little sprint and see how I do.' They all come out of the block intending to win. And that's how you need to view your dance school.

Hobby Vs Start up Vs Growth

Let's look at why you should do it.

Hobby – Are you doing it on the side of a full time job with no ambition to make it your full time job? Are you happy doing it this way? You will still need to abide by tax/business laws, but if you do not have an ambition to grow it past a few classes, you will still need to market the classes, budget them and ask if they are still breaking even. Just because it is not your primary source of income, it does not mean you should not be paid your worth.

Start Up – You have the passion and want to start a school, but you are really not sure how. You know you have to keep another job going until the school grows, but until then – where do you start? Where do the students come from? How does it run? Will people even come? What if it fails? (Cheeky PS – You NEVER fail, you ONLY learn). Remember when you learnt to ride a bike, and you had stabilizers first, and then when they came off you probably fell off a few times? Business is no different; pick yourself up, dust yourself off then –the bit that is not in the song – LEARN from it, then start all over again, this time putting into place what you did learn. I guess Dorothy Fields couldn't fit the learn bit in when she wrote the lyrics to that song!

Growth – You are serious about making money, doing what you LOVE and ONLY doing what you love! The foot-on-the-pedal growth period is crucial. This is where the safety blanket of 'the other job' gets taken away. Now you rely solely on the income of your school, so It HAS to work! It has to PAY! It HAS to be profitable.

But you see, this is where often the lines get confused. People often start up as a hobby, a bit of a side line and it maybe doean't have its breakeven and profit margins properly sorted, because it's 'only a few classes' – you may be getting to start to get the measure of me about the sentence 'it's only a few classes!' It's NOT only a few classes. It's a business....

Back to the thread...

The lines are confused, because the foundations are not clear. Iit was not set up properly in the beginning BECAUSE you were coming from a place of passion, because you led with your heart first and your head later. But now you have a problem, because dance schools in their nature need to grow. The kids grow. They learn, they develop skills, and they need harder classes, so now you need more classes, and it grows and grows and somewhere down the line, those lines become even more crossed, and before you know it, you are working for nothing.

Are you driven?

Are you ambitious?

Are you willing to take the calculated risks?

Is it in you?

Does your gut say, *I want more, I want to do this?*

Have you spotted a gap in the market? Are there opportunities?

Are you willing to do the homework, and get the foundations right? This book will REALLY help! (As will The Dance Den Membership.)

So what's your *why*, what is your driving force?

What is making you want to open this dance school?

This has to be super strong; 'I want to' is not going to cut it! Because when the s**t hits the fan, when things are not going right, you're driving force your what is what is going to keep you going. It's the thing that when you're ready to give up WILL keep you going. So what is your why? It has to be powerful enough.

Things like:

- My purpose is to bring quality dance classes to children who can't afford them.

- I want to bring dance classes to the masses.
- I want to have the next school that create stars.
- I want children to believe they can do anything they set their minds too, and dance is the start of that confidence.

What drives you?

WHY are you going to spend hours getting the foundation right, then hours marketing, hours prepping, hours teaching, hours on admin? Because you WANT this for you. Don't be afraid to say this! You want to be your own boss and that ladies and gentlemen if it is strong enough will drive you late into the night with ALL the passion you can muster! Just remember, lead with your head first.

Foundations are the core of everything

As teachers, we teach foundations day in, day out. Strong basic core techniques lead to rock solid foundations that will be the strength of any excellent dancer. So apply that to business. Get your foundations right and then move on from there. Or think of it another way, if you put building blocks up in a haphazard fashion and then try and build on top of them, the building will topple. Put strong foundations in place and the building can grow and be built up exponentially. Get it right from the start.

Here is a diagram that shows how the foundations all stack up on themselves, layering up to Dance School Growth.

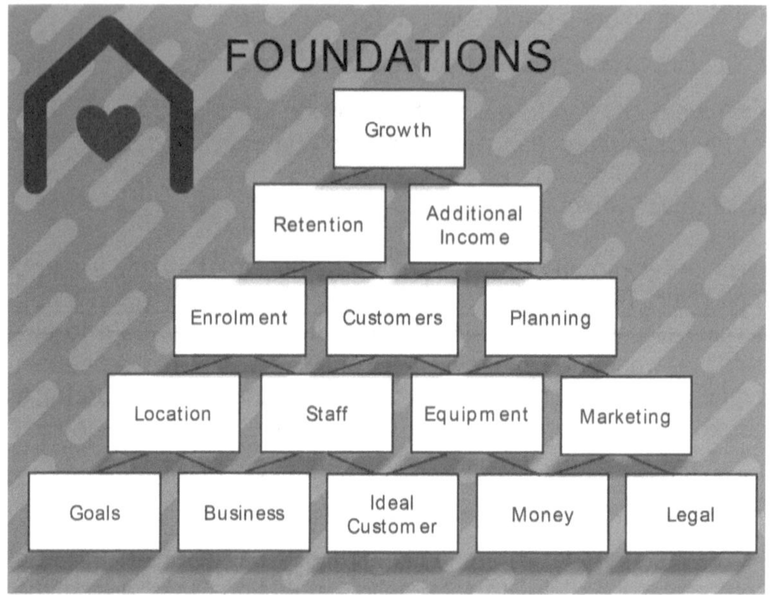

Summary

Understand your *why*, have a review of your skill set and see what is missing. What courses can you take, in what time scale, and what do you need to learn? Are you ready to take on the challenge?

If you really want to do something, you'll find a way.
If you don't, you'll find an excuse.

– Jim Rohn

Chapter 2

TAKING THE PLUNGE

Taking the plunge from employee to business owner

Perhaps you're thinking about it, but the reliability of your 'regular' wage is too much to give up? Let's get a little philosophical here. Imagine yourself at 60, never having opened your dance school, still working 9-5, and having to carry on till 67 or later to get your pension.

But ask yourself this question: *are you prepared to live with regret?* Because that's the biggest mistake anyone could make with their lives. Do not get to the point where you think, *I wish.* Wishing doesn't get you anywhere it's the same as worrying! Both are an empty space, both don't do anything for you! If you really want to set up the dance school then stop wishing and stop worrying. Get your arse in gear and get going!

I always wanted to write a book. So I've ticked that off my list. I refuse to get to 60 and regret. I have too many ideas and too much to give, and I'm sure you do too.

Yes, it takes courage, yes, it's scary, terrifying even, and you do have to put yourself out there and be prepared to be shot down. You have to step out of your comfort zone, and that's never easy. But it's also incredible! The confidence you gain, the self-belief – the 'you know what, yes I can do it and I'm good at it' realisation. Believe in yourself, take a deep breath – read this book!

Now for the maths...*Oh no, I hear you cry!* Later on in the book, I'll talk about break-evens, profit margins but right now I'm talking about survival. When I say survival – let's break this down:

Survival – This is the minimum that you need to survive. I'm not talking designer clothes, nail bars, or new cars. If you're going to do this, right now it's about replacing your basic living costs. Rent, bills, food, petrol – the essential basic living costs. Once you're established, then you can grow the business and move on/return to designer clothes and so on, but we need to do this step by step. Calculate your *basic* living costs for the month.

Basic survival monthly £'s, let's say for example that this figure is around:

£1000 x 12 months = £12,000

Divide this by 52 weeks of the year = £230.76 per week.

But dance schools don't run 52 weeks of the year. Most run anywhere between 33-46 weeks, because of holidays, Easter, Christmas etc. Therefore your true earnings have to be achieved in an average of 40 weeks.

£1000 x 12 months = £12,000

Divide this by 40 weeks of the year = £300.00

£300 per week is your basic survival; this is what you need in the bank to live.

Don't confuse this with what your dance school needs to earn. We will go into this in depth in the money chapter, but suffice to say your dance school has overheads such as insurance, hall hire, teacher hire, phones, stationary, music, tax – so your dance school has to earn £300 per week minus all ancillary costs.

So, for example, a ball park figure to aim for would be £350 per week (40 weeks of the year) just to survive.

Now you need to take the £350 and divide it by how many classes you realistically think you can start. Let's start small at four classes a week. That gives you £87.50 per class you would need to earn. With the average dance class costing £5 you would need 17.5 children in each of the four classes to break even.

For a new dance school, this is unrealistic, so you need to re-work the figures to make them do-able. Say you start six classes, that's:

£350 divided by 6 = £58.33

divided by £5 = 12 children per class.

That's much more realistic. Remember, we've also not taken into account any extra income revenue streams – more on this later. However, fundamentally you have to make the maths work at ground level.

I run 30 classes a week, over four evenings. Imagine if you didn't have your 9-5 job, how many classes could you start?

It is do-able, but you may need to do it in stages, and reduce your hours in your regular job as you build your dance school. Then, eventually replacing that income with revenue from teaching you'll be able to give up your full time job. You can do it, but you have to get the maths right first – you have to know what you are aiming for. Arm yourself with all the knowledge you can, get prepared and build your foundations first.

This chapter has so far assumed that you have a full time wage and you are looking to give up that security to run your own school. But you may be a teacher working for others and you've decided you want something yourself. You may be buying your previous teacher's school. There is more about 'getting' a school in chapter 5.

Let's make the assumption that you are a self-employed freelancer at the moment, and working for others, and you plan on continuing that whilst opening up your own school. Then survival costs are not going to be something to worry about so much, as you can probably keep that all going whilst you open; again on the assumption you don't burn your bridges!

Having been on the receiving end when a teacher has left to open her own school and students have followed: trust me, it hurts! We invested SO much of our time, passion, skills and energy in those students and when they go it can be seen as 'poaching'. Now poaching, although not illegal it is unethical and unmoral. Don't go there! If you are going to open a school in an area where you are already teaching, talk to who you teach for, do a different style dance or school, go to a different area. It is an unspoken rule in the professional industry and it's just not a good thing to do! Not only do you p off the support network around you, you also burn your bridges as far as survival income goes. You may also find that moving to set up a school in a different area would be much more beneficial as there may not be a school there, or close by. This book leads you through setting the dance school up right, going down the 'set up on the corner of another school and target their pupils' is not setting up a school right. Please let's be respectful of each other and the profession.

Never expect others to be like you. It can be the biggest nightmare! Collaboration and synchronization needs to be found in the difference.

– Harrish Sairaman

Mind-set

Let's get clear about your mind-set and what it takes to be your own boss. It involves courage and it takes strength. It's a chance for you to take control of your own destiny. It is also a risk, when I talk about risk, this is about calculated risk. It's about you understanding what you're getting into, not going bonkers but questioning, doing your homework and analysing what it is you need to do to give yourself the best chance of success. So yes, it takes courage.

To use the analogy: a ship is always safe at shore, but that is not what it was built for! What are *you* built for? What it boils down to is this: are you prepared to take a step in a direction that is going to change your life?

So think hard, take your time, dream and just go somewhere and think about what you truly want. These questions may help you:

- What do you see for your business?
- What does success mean for you?
- If money, people's opinions and my own fear were not a factor – what would I want?
- What do I need to let go to allow this?
- Why is success important to you?
- What difference does your business make?

If you are scared to make a decision – just make it! As one of my favourite social media pictures says: 'Right or wrong, just make a decision. The road of life is paved with flat squirrels who could not make a decision.' If five years down the road you situation changes and you no longer want the dance school, then that's fine – but that is five years down the line! Right now, you make the decision based on the facts you have in front of you.

So what is in front of you?

What is stopping you?

Don't be a flat squirrel!

Summary

Are you ready to make the change? This may take some time. Do your research, figure out what schools are in the area and find out what they are doing. Understand what your survival income will be and what you need to do to achieve that. Dream big, but research harder!

The man who moves a mountain begins by carrying away small stones.

– Confucius

Case Study

When I started my dance school, I was working a bar job, temping 9-5, and teaching in the evening and weekends. I quickly realised that as a barmaid I could earn £30 for five hours' work, when I could earn that in two hours teaching for someone else, or I could earn that and then some in one hour of my own classes. So I quickly gave up the bar work and got more teaching instead, and then I gave up the temp work, and then as my own classes grew, I gave up the teaching work that was not very well paid. Eventually, I gave up teaching for other people altogether.

One of the hardest decisions for me, and it was one of the last classes I gave up, was a job that brought me in £4000 a year for one day's work, 36 weeks of the year. It was a hard decision to drop that job, as I wondered how I would ever replace it. This may sound coy, but in reality I didn't miss it. In fact, it was one of the best things I ever did. It gave me more time to invest in my own business which naturally grew. I started new classes and doubled what I had given up. I took it step by step, replacing my income bit by bit.

Chapter 3

WHAT SCHOOL DO YOU WANT?

Ask yourself the right questions

Do your homework and get all the facts in front of you – that way you can make an informed decision.

What sort of school would you like to own? You could buy a franchise, lease, buy an existing or set up your own – let's look at the possibilities.

Established school

Positives

- Hopefully has a good reputation
- Has its own current students and database
- Already profitable
- It has a brand
- Has a relationship with its halls or has a venue
- Has teachers in place
- Has contacts to extra incomes
- Has contracts, accounts and insurance
- You don't have to do the hard work to set it up
- You are walking into a 'turnkey' business, which means it is ready to go!

Negatives

- You are buying a 'turnkey' business!

Which means that as a new principal, the current clients may not like any changes you bring about, such as price increases or changes of nights; the school may be reluctant to change. A dance school is a person-based business and the clients may not like you. This means that you might buy a school of 100, and they don't like the changes and suddenly you are left with 50. That would be a very different business form the one you just bought!

- The school has a bad reputation

There is a crossover that can be arranged, which can be written into contracts, where the leaving principal works and stays with the school for a set period of time to allow a smooth transition. The old principal would certainly have an emotional attachment to the school and will want to see it do well; the new principal would certainly not want to lose half its clientele in an instant. So it's in the best interests of both parties to arrange an amicable working agreement.

Conversation with a dance school owner who bought an established school

What's one piece of advice you'd give to a new start up who has bought a school?

Do not be afraid to establish who you are and the way you do things. You will lose students, but this is OK. You will gain more. It is important to not attempt to recreate what your predecessor had – they established the school, they ran the school in their way, but the only way to move successfully forward is to understand what to keep and what to change, and stick with it. Eventually you will stop hearing 'But Miss So-and-so did it this way,' trust me!

Why did you buy a school rather than starting your own?

I was in a position to take over a long-running school that would have closed had I not agreed to take over. The school was in my home village, and I had trained there as a child and teenager. It made perfect sense to me at the time to continue with what was already running and working.

Was the transition to you from the previous owner difficult?

I have learnt so many lessons during the last five years. The most important has probably been to trust myself, and be less afraid of what I have to offer. Taking over a business was more difficult than I had thought. I have inherited the good, the not-so-good, and the simply very different. And all of these things have proved challenging; how do I maintain the good, when I am not my predecessor, how do I fix the not-so-good, and how do I bridge the gaps between the various differences? After running the school predominantly as it was for the first two years I realised it was unsustainable for me and started to make changes that I had wanted to make, but had not up to then had the courage to make… These were some of the best management decisions I have made, and I regret not having made them sooner. After two or three stagnant years, the school's reputation is growing, the school is growing, the student experience is developing and our families are happy and excited to be part of our community. Trust in what you have to offer, and invest time in yourself, both personally and professionally so that you can be the best version of you, and the best leader you can be.

Mary O'Brien – Spotlight Dance School

Franchised school

When you buy a franchise you're buying a well-known brand, a proven formula and advertising, and ready with a support system in place.

Positives

- Proven to work
- Established brand
- Established structure
- Ready-made advertising

- Business support from head office
- Ready-made syllabus

Negatives

- Defined syllabus/structure offers less flexibility
- Costs to purchase franchise, (amount varies depending on brand recognition and strength of the franchise operation).
- An agreed percentage of your gross profit goes to franchise owner
- Limited flexibility

If you're thinking of getting a franchise, your first stop needs to be the British franchise Association https://www.thebfa.org/ There's also an exhibition you can attend with seminars that tell you all you need to know before investing in this type of business. As with everything in life, do your homework first!

Conversation with a dance school owner who bought a franchise:

One piece of advice to a new start up in your field (Franchise)

A franchise is in essence, a licence to operate a business using someone else's tried & tested methods. As a franchisee, you are required to follow certain methods as per the Licensor/Franchisor's instruction.

A franchise is great for those who have the passion to run a business in their specialist field but do not want to start from scratch. You have support every step of the way from the founders of the business, along with existing Franchisees who are usually willing to offer advice, support and will have experienced all of the new challenges you have or will face.

However, As a franchisee, you must be aware of where you stand. The franchisor owns the intellectual property (i.e. the logo, the name, copyright, business model, trademark etc.). If you decide to leave the franchise/sell/end your agreement, those clients will still be clients of the brand, not yours (i.e. if you leave your franchise and think you can approach your existing students to join your new school, you could face a lawsuit against you by the franchisor) even though you were the ones that found them.

You MUST be aware of Franchise Clauses that can enforce restrictions for a certain amount of time, if you decide to leave/sell and go forward with your own venture. Many franchisees who sell or leave sign an agreement to say that they will not engage in any business activity that is related to the model for a certain amount of time (usually one year).

As someone that has operated under a licensor's model for 5 years, I advise that you try to look at all of your options before committing. It is a MUST that you understand what a franchise is, and the terms of your franchise contract. I would highly recommend paying a solicitor to read through it before signing anything, and to have them explain the terms of the business you're about to devote all your time to. It's very easy to get caught up in the excitement of owning a readymade business, especially when you are passionate about the brand. However, it's when you've been operating for a while and become confident that knowing your rights becomes imperative. As you grow your business, your ambitions will grow too. You need to know what direction you can take your business in, and whether your ambitions fit into the franchisor's model.

Have you looked at starting your own school? What are you afraid of if you go it alone? Did you know that there are organisations that can supply funding and assistance to entrepreneurs? There are many services such as helping you with a business plan, cash flow and budget.

Why did you buy into a franchise?

I was lucky enough to not have to pay a franchise free for my Performing Arts School. However, even though there were other costs involved, I had seen existing branches operate whilst working as a teacher. I'd always wanted to run my own school, but looking back, I didn't feel knowledgeable enough in the compliance areas of running a business with children and vulnerable persons. I absolutely loved the model they had created, and was bursting with passion. Therefore, I wanted to be a part of that fabulous performing arts network.

Was it hard to get started?

Yes and no. I'd say it was daunting more than anything. I'd attended the principal training, and I had full support from head office, which created a full marketing plan for me. However, when you have boxes of 15,000 leaflets arrive at your door, you suddenly panic how you're going to distribute them all!

It's stressful, and I'm not going to say it was wonderful as 6 weeks leading up to my open day, I was miserable, questioning whether I could do it, and had those standard dreams of having two people turn up on the open day! However, once you've gotten it out of the way and done it, you now know how to open a theatre school! All of your marketing techniques can be analysed for next time. What did you do right? What could you improve on? What do you not need to focus your time on next time?

Dealing with parents is something that nobody can prepare you for until you've experienced it. Before becoming a principal, you just imagine the creative element to your wonderful new business. You don't think of dealing with parents who are needy, pushy, unorganised, and angry, or who have an issue with how you run your business. As much as I would like to say it won't happen, you will ALWAYS have to deal with parent issues. There are also the child protection standards you must adhere to, keeping good financial records, knowing how to manage your venues, teachers, enquiries etc.

However, once you experience it and crack it, you can achieve anything!

If you went back in time, would you do it again?

I am 50/50 on this. I cannot doubt that the experience I gained from being part of a network was priceless, and there were times I absolutely loved being part of such a successful and impressive brand. However, after looking back, I'm not sure I would advise my former self to take this route. It all depends on what you want to create in your school. You may want to do things your own way, which is absolutely great. Or, you may want to have guidance and support, which is also perfectly fine too.

When buying into a franchise, you'll need to pay a rather large franchise fee, which is often a minimum of £5-£10k. Some franchisors charge up to £15k just for the licence to operate; often this doesn't include working capital or your marketing budget etc. There are times that I just feel this amount of cash could easily set your own business up, where you could spend enough to create a steady, professional brand. Say if you have £10k, you could allocate £2k to marketing, £2k to initial teacher costs, £1000 for a professional website, logo design & branding, £2000 for a year's venue hire, £1000 for any memberships / first aid training / affiliations / advisory boards and another £1000 for equipment with £1000 spare. You've basically set yourself up with a professional business, which if it is done properly, will be a stable investment. Whereas, just spending £10k on a licence is dead money in my opinion. However, to those who don't want to go it alone. A Franchise Fee may be a worthwhile investment. It all depends on what is right for you!

Mark Bowman – Performer Workshop Ltd.

Licensed

To hold a license for a product is very different to a franchise, and some people get confused between the two. Zumba, Street Fit, Melody Bear – these are all types of licenses rather than franchises.

With a license, you attend training or buy a syllabus to be able to deliver the product. Once you have attended the training you can then use the name of the brand and run an unlimited amount of classes. There is normally a yearly subscription and top-up courses may be required, you may also have to order specific products like merchandising through their websites and then mark-up accordingly to your customers.

Positives

- You get training and a ready-made brand
- You can set any number of classes up
- Only a yearly subscription

Negatives

- Does not offer on-going business support
- Is a day course enough?
- Creative restrictions
- Must abide by specified terms and conditions

Conversation with dance school owners who bought a license for a product:

What are the benefits to buying a licence?

The benefits of buying a licence are the support network that you also get, such as lesson plans, marketing strategies and resources. Also, recommendations from other license owners and advice of what has or hasn't worked for them.

Would you buy a license again?

I have had two experiences, one of buying a franchise which I wouldn't do again, and recently having bought a license. I will be maintaining my licence for the foreseeable future with this particular package, as it has enhanced my dance school and provides a great resource too.

Karen Thompson – Karen Dempsey School of Dance

What are the negatives and positives to buying a licence?

On the positive side, music and choreography are supplied every month.

There are no negatives for me! This license has been worth every penny.

Was it hard to get started?

Not at all – I was sent a link to website with my email address and password to access which was set up on activation.

Would you buy another one?

If the license was similar to the current one and financially beneficial, then yes.

Kym Land – Katch Your Moves Academy of Dance and Fitness

Starting your own business

The world is your oyster; whatever you say goes!

Positive

- You can run it the way you want
- Name it, brand it, run it – your way
- Creative freedom
- Flexibility around your personal schedule

Negatives

- The buck stops with you
- There's always something to do
- Maintaining boundaries can be difficult
- Business acumen is required from day one
- Need to build a brand and get known to people

So, you've made the decision to open your own dance school or at least find out further information about what it all entails – excellent! Here are the next steps:

Conversation with a dance school owner who started their own school:

Give one piece of advice to a new start up in your field.

Truly understand your reasons for setting up. For example, your ethos of the business and your short and long-term goals. Be organised and plan.

If you could go back in time, what would you change?

I started in the days before automation and the amazing changes in technology, but I would look at reducing the hours I spent on administration and not be scared to outsource specific areas to other people. I still struggle with this a little but I am learning that I can't do it all and this doesn't make me a bad business owner.

Running a dance school has changed over time, how do you keep up?

I have always tried to keep up with ever-changing teaching methods and tried to remain aware of the latest trends. I teach ISTD syllabus work, therefore attending courses has been an important part of my professional development since I started teaching and is a great way to build a network of colleagues to discuss with and be inspired by.

What do you attribute to your longevity?

Tricky question! I suppose my refusal to give in, even at the low points during my business life. It can be difficult when teaching dance, as you give so much of yourself to others. Because of this we can often experience feelings of hurt if a situation arises which we can't resolve or if a negative comment is made about our business. I've learnt very good diplomatic skills and have become aware of the 'parent trap' as my career has continued. In recent years, I've learnt that a mentor can be an essential part of my business and personal development, especially as younger teachers use technology without thinking and have such different experiences nowadays, that it sometimes can feel overwhelming. However, an experienced dance studio owner and teacher has a wealth of knowledge and life experiences to pass on that should not be ignored therefore I continue to learn and develop.

Karen Thompson - Karen Dempsey School of Dance

Not for Profit / Charity School

Community based, potentially funded or an element of the school is charity based for outreach work

Positive

- You can access funding
- Name it, brand it, run it – your way
- You can have a massive impact on certain areas
- Flexibility around your personal schedule

Negatives

- Paperwork!
- Serious accountability as to HOW the funds are used
- There is normally a board of directors you need to get and listen too.
- Applications for funding are time consuming

Conversation with a dance school owner who set up a charity school:

What advice would you give to someone planning on setting up a charity?

The hardest thing about setting up a charity was finding a good bunch of people who would act as my board members and support my new venture. I also found it very difficult trying to understand all the paperwork that I had to complete with the writing of our constitution, although I have great help from Glamorgan Voluntary Services who guided me through each aspect and made sure it was exactly want I wanted. The waiting game was also hard. It took about six months for the reply from the Charity Commission to see whether my organisation had been accepted as a Charitable Incorporated Organisation. I decided to choose CIO rather than a company limited by guarantee or a CI Casa at the time I was establishing this new venture because many third sector companies were going into administration due to the lack of funding. By becoming a CIO it allows me to tap into more trusts for grant funding. We only have to prepare one set of accounts which, as this was one of my weak areas, I thought was the best option.

Are there still pots of funding available?

Yes there are still some pots of funding in 2018, but you have to be innovative with your projects to be successful. You also cannot rely on being awarded funding in today's climate so your business has to sustain itself – if we get funding it's a bonus!

The advice I would pass on to someone wanting to set up their dance school as a charity would be that you have to make sure everything you do is for the benefit of the public, not yourself – so I am an employee of the charity – I do not own it! Be prepared to go months without getting paid a director's wage and yet still wear all the hats in the studio. But as long as you have a board of experienced and skilled members who can support you, it does help. I have seen a growth in my business since 2015 when we registered as a CIO, and I believe it was the right choice. If you are passionate about making a difference to lives, then becoming a charitable organisation is the best option – if you want to remain working as a sole trading company getting profits then you may want to choose another legal status for your business.

Emma Malam – E- Motion Dance Company

Style

The next decision is what type of school you choose to run, whether specialist, exam-based or non-exam-based. To make it easier, I've broken a number of ideas down into a chart below. Some dance teachers reading this are qualified through an examining body and may want to continue with their syllabus/exams. Others may need a bit of inspiration.

Specialist	Exam	Non Exam
Ballet – RAD, ISTD, Checetti	ISTD	Street
Irish / Highland – Folk based	RAD	Community / Creative
Street	BTDA	
	UKA	
	UDO – Street	
	Numerous others...	

I'm making an assumption about training here. this book is about opening a dance school, and with that comes the need for a highly specialised skill. If you're not trained as a dance teacher, I would advise you contact either Dance UK (https://www.danceuk.org/) or CDET (http://www.cdet.org.uk/) for further training information and examining bodies.

Of course, there is the possibility to mix and match – it's your school, your way. So to give an example – say you opened a Street school:

Example: Street School

You could base this on style and run individual locking, popping, waaking, break classes (the only drawback would be the access to good teachers), and then add in the street exams as an extra.

Alternatively, you could run generic street classes, adding on specialist style courses and leave out the exams.

Example: Exam-based school

Run tap, modern, ballet classes within the exam structure but also run complementary non-exam based street classes. At least you are offering variety as not everyone would want street or exams. Running both an exam and recreational stream does mean you are attracting two types of clients with double the income opportunities.

Summary

Understand the type of school you want to run. There are so many options out there that would give you a HUGE helping start. Do your homework, get researching online. Look at what other dance schools in the UK and abroad are doing, get inspiration. Contact people, visit their classes, ask questions…forewarned, forearmed.

The secret of getting ahead is getting started!

– Mark Twain

FOUNDATION AND SET UP

Chapter 4

GOALS

Goals

Goalsetting is like satellite navigation. If you wanted to drive to Scotland would you do it without knowing where you are going? Without a satnav you could end up in Wales or it might take you three times as long to get there! So it's about having a focus and an end result in place, a direction to go so that you don't get side-tracked, or distracted by, as I like to call it, the shiny shiny! The 'shiny shiny' is all the little things that attract you and pull you off focus. So let's just say you are on Facebook to do some marketing, but then a cat video comes up, and you decide to watch that because it looks funny, and then because the algorithms on Facebook are very, very clever, they decide that you like cats and you would probably like to see more cats! Those cat videos could be two or three minutes long, and before you know it 10 to 15 minutes of your day have gone on watching cats, and now your news feed is now full of cat videos!

It's very easy to get lost on Facebook. I have a very vocal love-hate relationship with it so it is really about focusing getting your head down doing the work. When you have really strong goals then those goals will drive you. It is then about taking those goals breaking them down into a plan and then acting on them.

When it comes to goals it's about setting them. Write them down and make plans to achieve them – that's all there is to it! There is nothing magical about it BUT get it wrong and it can make anything seem overwhelming or unsurmountable. Get it right and it not only raises your confidence, it also drives your business forward & fast.

So the steps to goal setting are:

Dream it!

Break it down!

Time it!

Do it!

Step 1- Dream it!

Let your mind wander

Dream it Questions

- What do you see for your business?
- What does success mean for you?
- If money, people's opinions, and fear were not factors – what do I want?
- What do I need to let go to allow this?
- What do you want your business to become? List – Pupils, numbers, events, staff, studios....
- Why is success important to you?
- What difference does your business make?
- Why did you start or want to start?
- What do you want to do each day?
- How many hours do you want to teach?
- Who do you want to work with – core focus?
- What income do you want?
- What are your core values?
- What do you want in your life?
- How will your life goals fit with your business goals?

Step 2- Break it down

There are a couple of steps to break down your vision / dream.

First, you need to get it out of your head and somewhere visual, written goals are much more statistically likely to work than those in your head.

Try these options:

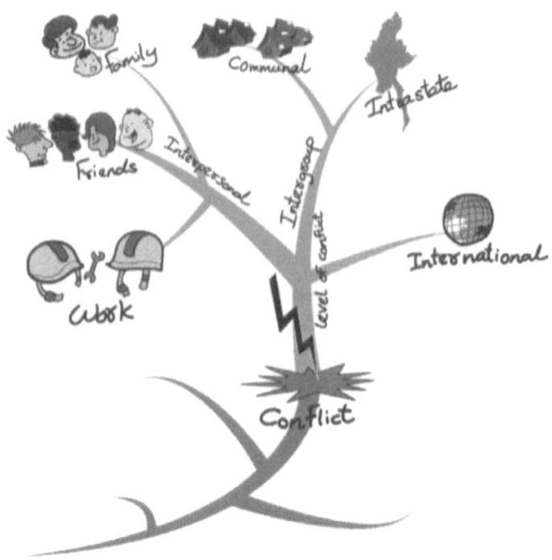

Mind map:

This is my personal favourite. The lines stem out from the centre into organised chunks.

Vision Board:

Time to get all Blue Peter; get creative with the magazines and sticky tape.

Brain Dump:

Doesn't matter how... just get it out of your head so that your brain has room to move, think and dream.

Second, clarify those dreams and give them a focus, maybe try splitting the areas down into:

Personal – I want a three bedroom house with drive, I want a Ferrari, I want x holidays per year

Business – I want a building for a studio, I want x pupils, I want x income

Be specific about your goal. Generalisation is not enough, if you want a Ferrari, specify what colour, what make, and by when!

Step 3- Time it

This is crucial!

There is a goal setting tool (there are numerous ones) but this is my personal favourite called SMART. (Commonly attributed to Peter Drucker's **Management by Objectives** concept. The first known use of the term occurs in the November 1981 issue of *Management Review* by George T. Doran. Credit: Mindtools.com)

Smart helps you set your goals:

S – Specific

M – Measured

A – Attainable

R – Realistic

T – Timely

Going back to the Ferrari, if you are earning £100 a week and you want to buy one by next month – it is not realistic, not attainable and not timely. This is the sort of goal that would get you overwhelmed, despondent and would often make you say 'why do I bother?' The same goal, eight or ten years down the line when you have multiple studios and a six-figure income, becomes a goal that can drive you.

Step 4- Do it!

But how?

Answer: Work backwards!

If you start with the goal, let's take buy a pint of milk as an example:

Buy milk

Go to shop

Write list

Earn money

Work

You would start with working to earn the money, writing your shopping list, heading to the shop and buying the milk. If you started with buying the milk, you may get there and have no money! So you have to build it in order.

Put it in order to do it step by step. It's easier to work it backwards, to start at the goal and work your way to where you are today. Break it down into years, months and days, and break it down to the extent where it is bite sized.

Goals should not overwhelm you. They need to be big enough to drive you, but not so big that they scare you.

Summary

Take time out to dream and plan your goals. Run it by someone if it helps – they can check if they are big enough, achievable and if you can realistically manage them. Review your goals regularly, every 3 months or so to ensure you are on track, but make sure you set them!

A goal should scare you a little and excite you a lot

– Joe Vitale

Chapter 5

BUSINESS

Business

When you set yourself up as a business, you need to decide what sort of business type you are, ignoring corporations and large scale business, as a dance school is unlikely to ever fall into these categories. You will be either self-employed as a sole trader, set up a company, a limited company or a partnership.

My advice at this point is to follow the link to: **https://www.gov.uk/business-tax/self-employed**

This is the government site for business, and it can help guide you with all elements of self-employment, and it is up-to-date. It also has all the information you need on National Insurance contributions, tax, expenses, self-employed assessment and so on. My advice is not to be scared off by all the talk of 'ltd' and so on, it's not at all as scary as it may seem. If it does really confuse you, then look for further help, get an accountant or a bookkeeper – what you pay them will save you in the long run. The government has business support helplines https://www.gov.uk/business-support-helpline these can direct you to your local business support network and give you access to a business advisor.

Also sign up to www.thedanceden.co.uk. Although this community of dance school owners are not qualified accountants, we are all living and breathing the very business operation you want to start. What better place to get help than from experienced business owners?

Business plan

So, here is where I go against all the advice I've given before. Business plans; all the advisors will tell you that you need them. I am telling you don't! Well, not a full one anyway, unless that is you are applying for a business loan, then the bank will need one. But you do need an understanding of the market you are entering, a financial plan, marketing objectives and clear goal setting. Have a look at the chart below:

STANDARD BUSINESS PLAN	NEED	DON'T NEED	SARAH'S PLAN
Executive summary: mission statement, vision and purpose		X	Mission statement: I wrote one 16 years ago and have never used it. Vision and purpose: I think you know that already! What you will need to know is your why!
Target market – who is your product destined for, demographic, interests and budgets	X		The 'who' is really important. This is identifying your ideal customer (more on this later) the rest not really important because if you get your IC (Ideal customer) right, the rest will follow.
Market analysis – means a study of the other dance schools around your area	X		A study of your competitors is essential so you can emulate what they do well and avoid what they do poorly. An understanding of their pricing structure is also important.
Human resources – staff, payments and contracts	X		You will need this if you plan on hiring straight way, it's irrelevant if it's just you.
Services – halls, suppliers	X		You don't need to plan for venues, but you need them! Suppliers not necessarily so, you can supply dance wear, uniform at a later date.
Marketing – how do you get the message out there?	X		This is crucial for your business survival. You'll need a mix of offline and online and you'll need to plan this in advance
Operations – how do you plan on achieving the task?		X	You need the right mind-set and clear goal setting (more later).

STANDARD BUSINESS PLAN	NEED	DON'T NEED	SARAH'S PLAN
Financials – how much money you need and profitability. Profit and Loss.	X		Hopefully, you've done your maths on the start-up costs, profitability and growth (more later). Profit and loss (knowing the figures, breakeven and profitability) is essential.

The mistake that I made, and which a lot of new dance school owners make, was downloading a standard business plan, and trying to make it work. The truth is our businesses do not necessarily fall into the 'standard' category. So don't try to fit into a template, make your own plan a roadmap to your new start, your dream business. And now the fun starts!

Let's make a plan:

1.

What is your *why*? I asked you this earlier in the book, so re-write it here. Your why is what drives you, so it needs to be at the forefront of everything you do.

_ _

_ _

_ _

_ _

1a.

Add in goals. What is your aim for the first year; what is your vision and target?

2.

Your ideal client. This I cover in the next chapter, so when you have completed it come back and write it here:

3.

Market analysis. There is not enough room here for the types of in-depth research you will need to do. However, once you have done it, collate the results here:

Dance School 1 (Name) ____________________________

Strengths

- ____
  ____
  ____
  ____

Weaknesses

- ____________________________________

Dance School 2 (Name) __________________________

Strengths

- ____________________________________

Weaknesses

- ____________________________________

Dance School 3 (Name) __________________________

Strengths

- ____________________________________

Weaknesses

- ______________________________________
  ____
  ____
  ____

Dance School 4 (Name) ____________________________

Strengths

- ______________________________________
  ____
  ____
  ____

Weaknesses

- ______________________________________
  ____
  ____
  ____

What is missing from the area?

____

____

____

____

What type of dance school do I like? What excites me?

____

____

____

____

Is there money to be made? (Have you done the maths?)

____

____

____

____

What would make me different from the other dance schools?

____

____

____

____

4.

Human resources: What is it you need to get your business off the ground? Designers, website development, resources, financial help, business advisor, a mentor? Make a list of the help you will need.

5.

Make a list of the suppliers you need to source. Halls, dancewear, prop purchases, music.

6.

Marketing. This is covered in detail later in the book. Draw a few doddles here of any ideas you have for a logo, strap line, thoughts for marketing and how you can get the message out there.

7.

Operations. What is your launch date?

OPENING DATE:

_ _ / _ _ / _ _ _ _

Now get on and get going!

8.

Financials. Come back and write this in here when you have read the chapter.

What is your survival cost? £ _ _ _ _ _ _ _ _ _ _ _

What is your break even costs? £ _ _ _ _ _ _ _ _ _ _ _

How much profit will you make on each class? £ _ _ _ _ _ _ _ _ _ _ _

How much money will you make in your first year? £ _ _ _ _ _ _ _ _ _ _ _

Summary

I cannot stress enough the importance of doing your homework. Asking questions, lots of them! Visit people and get an idea of 'how' they do it. It is not until you talk to people so you really understand the areas that the polished marketing material does not tell you.

Research is formalized curiosity. It is poking and prying with a purpose.

– Zora Neal Hurston

Chapter 6

THE IDEAL CUSTOMER

Picture your perfect student and perfect parent. I mean the type that hang on your every word; they don't question, they fully support, and they're prepared to pay without complaining for shoes, leotards, branded merchandise, extra lessons, private lessons, costumes and so on... OK, so back to reality....Are you really going to get a school full of those types of clients? Of course not. But you can get close. By being crystal clear on who you want as a customer, what your expectations are, what your rules are and through coherent and consistent branding and advertising you will attract the right type of customer.

TASK – answer the following questions

What problems will you solve for them?

How do you make their life easier?

What are they looking for?

What do I do really well for them?

What is missing in your area/dance school?

What should make them choose you?

Is your communication up to scratch?

How do you help them?

How do you meet a need?

Who is your dream student?

Who is your dream parent?

What are you NOT delivering to attract your dream student?

Once you have answered all the questions above and have figured out who your ultimate students are – NOW choose six words that evoke the kind of customer experience that you want to create and which you can use in your advertising.

YOUR empowered words

1. ....
2. ....
3. ....
4. ....
5. ....
6. ....

Now with that dream student segment sorted lets define them down even further so that eventually you come up with a more targeted solution.

S.E.S FORMULA

Customer Segments

A customer segment, also known as an ideal client or customer avatar, is a way for you to understand your consumer, so that when you write your marketing, you can be specific about WHOM you are targeting. In dance schools, the more you can segment these down into smaller, more niched sections, the better your marketing will work. In most dance schools you would have a number of customer segments.

Break your dance school down into smaller sections based on one of the three segments below.

STYLE

- Ballet, Tap, Modern, Street, Freestyle, Ballroon, Theatre, Jazz, Acro

AGE

- Baby classes only, Adults, under 8's etc......

STRUCTURE

- Exams only, Competition only, Non Exams, medals etc......

My Dance School

EXAMPLE	SEGMENT 1	SEGMENT 2	SEGMENT 3	SEGMENT 4
Ballet				

Now further niche the segment down by using one of the other sections, you may need to repeat this process.

My Dance School

EXAMPLE	SEGMENT 1	SEGMENT 2	SEGMENT 3	SEGMENT 4
Ballet				
Baby Class				

So for example: If I was a ballet only school, I would need to segment my school down into age categories – baby ballet, Fairy Ballet, seniors.......

Or a Street school may have broken their segments into styles then ages.

You need to mix and match this, until you have found the perfect combination of segments.

With the segments and your ideal student pictured, you now know WHO you will be targeting with your marketing, who you want to attract to your school and who will be enticed by your branding.

Name

What's in a name? Everything is my response! You have outlined your ideal customer, you know who you want to attract. So, let's ask these questions. Think about the sustainability of your dance school – is this something you plan on selling on in the future or passing on to your children? If so, is the Joe Bloggs School of Dance an appropriate moniker?

TASK

What are your core values?

What are your ethics?

What do you represent?

If you are a strong, honest, passionate yet technically driven teacher, a name like 'Happy Dance' would not represent who you are. Think hard on your name: there may be a very personal reason as to why you name it what you do – one friend of mine named her dance school after her mother, whom she lost at an early age; but think hard, this name will stay and grow in stature and reputation, therefore it needs careful consideration.

It needs to be memorable

Does the school name describe what you do? This sounds basic, even like I'm insulting your intelligence... but I've seen dance schools who name themselves so oddly that you question when looking what exactly they do?

Even if it's initials, such as the ABC dance school, make sure it has 'dance school' or 'the academy', something that demonstrates you teach dance.

A few things that may help you:

- Named after a dance move
- Something inspirational
- Initials

A few things you should avoid

- Naming it after the street the building is on:

  (What happens if you need to move or if the street name is inappropriate?)

- Using a word that means something else in another culture or language or slang

- Naming it similar to a local competitor:

  Lacks professionalism

  The public will get confused between the two of you

  Your reputation will be linked to theirs, with potentially disastrous consequences

So be bold, be different, think hard and test! Then test again! Not just on your family as they will potentially say 'Oh, that's lovely,' regardless of what they really think. Get out into the public, do some old fashioned market research with a clip board and five options and ask then to put them in order of preference. If you're more hi-tech run a survey using survey monkey (https://www.surveymonkey.com).

If you run a survey on Facebook, be sure to follow Facebook rules and regulations.

There is a bonus to doing it the old-fashioned way. Your competitors won't find out what you are doing! Your launch needs planning and a big wow factor. And not all dance school owners are honest, and some may sabotage you before you begin. This is not something I feel comfortable saying, but unfortunately, as with every business sector, there are some sharks out there.

Branding

Now you have your name, it's time to think on your colours, your logo and the overall look of the company. What colour stands out to you and works with what you represent? Think about colours that stand out really well. When I first started my school I used white and light blue and a small logo. In hindsight that just blended in, I was trying to hide the fact I had created this new school, not scream it from the rafters. In this day and age, competition is tough and you need all the help you can to stand out.

When you get your branding right it will really help your business. Your vision, what you want and what you offer from the school – all of that – will be cleverly integrated into a logo and a strap line. Think about it this way, this is the first contact that your customer has visually of what you do and what you offer so it has to be right. The right branding will highlight what makes you different or makes you more desirable.

Things to think and more importantly what you will need to give to a designer.

Your vision – what do you see your dance school being about? Is it about excellence? Is it about inclusion? What is your vision for the future of your dance school?

You – what is your personality all about? Every dance school will be different because of who leads them. I often say a dance school is a product of its owner. So what is it about you, that brings something special to the dance school?

Them – what will the business achieve for its customers?

Colour:

There is much more to it than picking a colour that you really like, although remember you are likely to live with this for years, so if you can't stand black then potentially don't use it. There is a whole psychology to the use of colour in branding so for example:

Yellow = optimism

Blue = trust, dependability and strength

Orange = friendly and cheerful

There is a whole spectrum and range of meanings and emotions that go with choosing a colour.

Font

As with colour there is a science behind the use of font in your brand. Every font has a unique personality and characteristic, so choose one that best reflects how you want your dance school to be represented

For example:

Serif font = traditional and reliable

Script fonts = elegant and classical

If you decide to go with a design company they will build your brand for you. They will sit with you and understand what the business is about, what you want and what your vision is for the company. From there they will build you a number of examples and you can develop the brand together until you are happy

Imagine your pupils walking around the shops in your branded merchandise; without being disrespectful to them, they are walking advertising. Make sure that the branding works for you in the right way!

Logo

As creative people, you may well have been doodling away and have come up with a design already, or have an idea of how you want it look. If you don't then try a Google Images search. Don't copy what you find, but it may well inspire you. Or alternatively give free reign to your designer and see where they take you.

If money is an issue:

TOP TIP

Use Fiverr (https://www.fiverr.com). On this site you can get a logo created for $5 which is about £3.80. You may need to use a few designers to get it right, as with all types of these services there are some muppets and some amazing experts. So be prepared, that £3.80 may become £15. Either way, £15 is not a lot of money for a logo.

Summary

There are lots of things in this chapter. You need to look at who your ideal customer/student is and segment them down so they will be easy to market to. Plus the element of a school name and branding, which should all tie in to who you are trying to attract. Lots of work, but if there was one chapter that I would want you to spend time on – it would be this one!

"Focus on building the best possible business. If you are great people will notice and opportunities will appear"

– Mark Cuban

Case Study

When I rebranded my dance school after 16 years, I went to a reputable local company. Yes, it cost me more money than fiverr.com but I had felt for years that my logo had been miss representing what I stood for. I knew what my company was about, I knew what we represented, I knew what I wanted and I had demonstrated this for 16 years, but my branding absolutely did not reflect that.

The question that has come up in the Dance Den and has often been asked of me, is that as dance school owners is it OK to rebrand? Some are scared to make the jump. Rebranding and new branding, when it's done right, will only enhance and help your business, because now what you do and what you're about is truly represented in a single image.

When I rebranded, all the feedback I got was excellent, everyone loved it. Not only that, my business has improved because of it. Now it stands out and 'says what it does on the tin!' In an instant people understand what my school is about.

In contrast, when I was getting the logo together for the Dance Den, I went to numerous designers on fiverr.com and no matter how clear I was with my instructions, they never seem to really get what I was about or what I wanted to achieve.

In the end I launched the business with a hastily put-together logo that I wasn't happy with and within the year it had changed. The new one lasted two years and again it didn't represent me and what I was about. So again I went to the same company, and yes it cost me more money than the cheap sites, but the results were incredible. I should have gone to them in the first instance. I cannot underestimate the importance of your designer knowing you your vision, what you stand for and how important that is. So really work to get it right from the start.

Chapter 7

MONEY

Money

It's so important to know your numbers. How many students you have in the classes, how much income you have, any bad debts there are, your cash flow and your break-evens.

Cash flow

This is what keeps you going year in, year out. Given that I mentioned earlier an average dance school is 40 weeks of the year, you have to be paid 52 weeks of the year. So what you earn in that 40 weeks has to last you across the whole year.

My top tip is to develop excellent financial management skills. If you earn £20 you need to allow 20% for tax/NI, so that gives you £16, so allow yourself £8, and that way the remainder soon adds up for your wage on the weeks you are not working.

Number of students

You should continually be monitoring how many students you have in each class. This gives you a good guide for which classes need more marketing, which ones are not working at all, which are the really popular ones (and you can then schedule more of the most popular classes).

Bad debt

Realistically this should not happen. Where possible, parents should be encouraged to pay online; it will save you so much hassle. Chasing payments is a big thing, so from the start you need to decide on your policy. You have a number of options.

1. Have an early bird booking system, if they pay before a certain date they get x% back or a £5 credit, a free class or a secure place. In a highly competitive market, I find securing a place hard to maintain as ultimately you do not want to lose that student. So some kind of incentive is great.

2. Late payment fee. Yep, this one works, but it doesn't work if you don't uphold it! Stick to your guns and charge it.
3. Incentives for paying direct debit or online. A business account with most banks will charge fees for cheques and cash handling, so when you do your sums on the internet, you may find they work in your favour. And when you calculate your time into the equation for checking, data entry and a trip to the bank, I am sure you will find the internet is the way forward.

Break-evens and profit margin

Grab a cup of tea, this is about to get mathematical!

Your breakeven is the figure you need to achieve so that you do not lose money.

Profit margin and mark up often get confused but they do pretty much mean the same thing. Profit is the figure that you are left with after you have taken away costs. Mark-up is the figure you would add to your base cost. So if a cup of tea costs 20p to make, when you sell it at £1, your profit margin is 80p before tax. They are basically the same, it's just that mark-up is often dealt with in percentages.

Before getting too technical – the BIG numbers you need to know are your break-evens:

To find a breakeven:

First your costs on a single dance class:

ITEM	£
Hall	10 an hour
Teacher	20 an hour
Total	30

Add on your auxiliary costs (example)

If you're not sure – get a quote and use that or at least a guess, you can adjust later.

ITEM	£	YEAR	WEEK
Insurance	600	600	11.54
PPL (Music Licence)	90	90	1.73
Music		500	9.61
Stationery	10 per week	520	10
Travel			50
Expenses			20
TOTAL			102.88

Other items you need to include are – your time doing administration (yep, that counts too), bank charges, electric, heating, phone, broadband add it all in!

Multiply your auxiliary costs by the number of weeks you hold dance classes:

102.88 x 40 weeks = £4115.20

Multiply the number of classes you do per week by the number of weeks you teach:

10 classes per week x 40 weeks of the year = 400 classes per year

Divide your total auxiliary costs by the total number of classes :

£4115.20 divided by 400 classes = £10.29

£10.29 represents the total figure your auxiliary costs cost you per class.

Take your class total and add on auxiliary costs:

£30

+ £10.29

= £40.29

£40.29 add on tax at 20% = £48.34

£48.34 represents the total amount of money you need to take in one class to break even.

An average price of £5 a class means you would need 10 children to just break even.

Add on another 10 children, so you have 20 in the class, then you make a profit before tax of £50.

So if you want a 50% profit margin on a single class then you would need to have 15 children in every class you teach.

If you apply this formula to everything you do – shows, events, workshops, costumes, merchandise, clothing, and all classes then you will know your figures and what is working and what's not. If your breakeven point is 18 per class and that is unrealistic, then you are both charging too little and need to put up your prices AND you need to bring down your costs. Do not just bring down your costs, you are in business to make money, and if you only bring down costs, there will come a point sooner than you think where costs will increase and you will be back to losing money.

This is a business, not a hobby.

This is where it gets interesting.

If your breakeven point is 10

And the price per class is £5

Adding 2 more children in a class = £10 a week or £100 a term (10wk term) or £300 a year (3 term year)

Adding 5 more children in a class = £25 a week or £250 a term (10wk term) or £750 a year (3 term year)

Adding 10 more children in a class = £50 a week or £500 a term (10wk term) or £1500 a year (3 term year)

If you do this with 3 classes you would gain an additional £4500 a year! PROFIT!

Dance Schools have the potential – but you MUST know your numbers, and which classes are making you the money. Do more of these. Which ones are not, and why? There are any numbers of reasons why a class may not be making money, but it is your job to figure out why, fix it and plug the hole that is losing your business money.

Summary

Don't get stressed about the numbers, but as soon as you know HOW, it is so important to keep the consistency up. Create yourself an excel sheet and plot them all in, that way it is easy to reference and update them.

Be aware of little expenses. A small leak will sink a great ship.

– Benjamin Franklin

Chapter 8

LEGALITIES

Legalities

Here we go......

Insurance

Every dance school needs public liability insurance. If you have staff, even if they are freelance workers, you will also need employers' liability. Some venues may ask to see a copy of your certificate, and regardless of this your certificate should be on display, even if you rent the building.

If you are a member of an association, you can get your insurance through them, and there are specialist companies out there specialising in creative businesses. It's also worth pointing out that you need to check your insurance – be honest and upfront. I once had an insurance policy that did not cover shows! I had to get a separate insurance for that, so make sure that the insurance company you go with understands all the elements of your business.

PPL + PRS

There is often confusion over which licence you will need, and in some instances you will need both – for example, for shows – but as a freelance dance teacher you will definitely need PPL.

My advice here is to go straight to the source – follow the link, explain what you are doing, include your shows and ask relevant professional people which licence you need in which situation.

http://www.prsformusic.com/users/businessesandliveevents/pages/differencebetweenprsformusicandppl.aspx

As for insurance, I can't stress enough the importance of being honest and upfront. This is not the area where you scrimp and become an Ebenezer; because this is crucial and you do not want to be landed with a bill for £1000s because you tried to save £20 by missing out some information!

First Aid

Although a first aid certificate is not compulsory, I wish it was. At the very least given that you are working with children you will need a basic level, and some places offer the paediatrics addition to the basic and I believe this is worth getting too.

There are lots of providers in your area running relevant courses:

Child Protection Course

This is worth doing as the more knowledge you have as a teacher of children the better. (Also see the note under the chaperone license). Local councils/ training providers and universities all run a number of short courses and qualifications on child protection.

Disclosure and Barring Service (DBS)

Previously known as the Criminal Records Bureau or CRB, this is the certificate that you need to work with children, and you need the advanced version. It proves that you have not engaged in any criminal activity in the past. As a dance school owner, all your freelancers should have one and should have given you a copy of it on acceptance of their job. If any activity shows up on the DBS it is then your decision as a dance school owner whether to hire that person or not.

You can get these online from https://www.ddc.uk.net

Your associations may also be able to get one for you.

Chaperone licences

Technically, as the dance school owner you do not need this, because when you run a show, it is unlikely you are 'responsible' for the children. What I mean by this is that although you are ultimately responsible for their safety and wellbeing, for the purpose of running a show that 'chaperone' job is something you should have delegated.

However, that said, I do have one. As councils get tougher on vocational schools and their legalities, in my eyes it is imperative that you, all your staff and all your parents 'helping' backstage have one. As I write, my local council will do spot checks on licences and can shut your show down without the correct paper work. Ignorance is not a defence!

Check with your council what their requirements are. At the time of writing this, (2018), my council legally requires me to have:

Ages 8 and under: One licenced chaperone to every eight children

Ages 9 +: One licensed chaperone to every 12 children

Please check with your council as it may vary.

I personally don't think that is enough for my babies (ages three-five). I have one licensed chaperone to every three children for that age group.

For my shows, the only people allowed backstage are chaperones with licences. A volunteer licence (which is free in my council) requires a DBS, child protection course and proof of identity. This way I know all of my students are in safe hands.

Now this is where the waters can get muddy!

As a parent you have a right to chaperone your own child without a licence! Therefore, you can have a room full of licenced chaperones and one unlicensed. It's bonkers! Seriously, this drives me insane!

Gah, don't get me started! But the end result is that you have to allow that parent backstage! End of story!

I get around this by requiring all parents to have licences, and I only allow a small percentage of unlicensed people backstage. Otherwise you just have too many mums back there. It's also worth noting here, that legally you need a separate changing room for male members, and a male licensed chaperone for them.

So why have I gone off on a tangent about chaperones here and not in the show section? Well there is more to come, this is a huge subject and one that can very easily go wrong. But it's here for its legalities – if you apply for a chaperone licence, you get your child protection course and your DBS. Which could potentially save you a lot of money.

BOP licence

On the subject of shows a BOP licence is required from the council on any performance that involves children. Contact your local council about this, it does relate to the chaperone licenses and each council will run theirs slightly differently. Go to the source.

Data protection

The information commissioner's office has a very comprehensive website where you can take a short test to see if you need to register yourself on the data protection register. Even if you don't, you will still need to abide by the data protection act, so please use the website and learn directly from them what is involved.

https://ico.org.uk

Coming into force in 2018 (and the second edition of this book) are the new GDPR rules; use the following link to make sure that you are compliant with the new rules.

https://ico.org.uk/for-organisations/guide-to-the-general-data-protection-regulation-gdpr/

POLICIES

Your company should hold policies on:

- Child protection
- Health and safety
- Social media
- Customer care
- Complaints procedure

There is a short cut to these – so don't panic!

I recommend you register your School with CDET (Council for Dance Education and Training). They have a recognised school status and inclusion in their register requires you to be qualified and have your policies, insurance, DBS, First Aid and everything I have mentioned in the preceding points. You need these to set yourself up as a legitimate school. They have examples you can use on their site and this will help you. It does cost to gain recognised status, so if money is tight at the moment, then go ahead and get your policies in place anyway. This won't cost you anything in the short term and you will need them.

By checking through your policies, you will also get a clearer understanding of what is acceptable and what is not. Spend time on your complaints procedure, customer care and social media.

Think about some of these questions as you write these policies:

Complaints

You will get them so be prepared for them.

- What do you deem an acceptable complaint?
- Face to face?
- Email only?
- Do you have a two or three stage procedure?
- What is your follow up?

Customer Care

- How do you make them a raving fan?
- How can you make your processes as easy as possible?
- Are all your staff on the same page?
- Are you pleasant, and do you listen well?

Social media

This is a biggie! Think hard!

- Do you find it acceptable for a mum to post pictures of your dance class?
- Do you find it acceptable to be criticised?
- Do you allow videos?

Please think on this very hard! As I've said, I have a very vocal love-hate relationship with social media; it can and *will* bite you when you least expect it. Please trust me when I say it will come back at you. So be tough from the start – bite that proverbial bullet and protect your ass! Don't think it won't happen to you, because it can. Therefore, protect yourself as much as you can, put your boundaries in place of what you deem acceptable and then make them stronger! Review this policy frequently!

Dance Schools – personal forms

Terms and Conditions

Things to think about for this document are your procedure and policy on issues such as payment, merchandise, dance wear, class etiquette, registration, liability, class cancellation, and permissions for filming and photography. There needs to be a signature at the bottom and then they need to be stored correctly according to the Data Protection Act.

But let's just stop a second and think about something. As humans we always think that something bad is going to happen to someone else, we never think it will happen to us. But, and this is a massive but, as much as you don't want to think it, you have to take it into account. This chapter is all about getting the solid fundamentals right, because although it may not be something really bad, there will be times when you are faced with problems. Nine times out of ten, these problems can be pre-empted and prevented if you have clear communication, procedures and rules in place that your customers (i.e., your pupils' parents) are clear about. Think about things and situations before they actually happen; ask yourself the question – if x,y,z was to happen, what would be the policy on how to deal with this? Then use that to inform your terms and conditions.

Other forms you will need:

- Enrolment form and risk assessment.

Other forms you will need to consider writing are:

- Show handbook – a guide to all your expectations and rules when putting on a show.

- Welcome handbook or letter – eliminating fears and questions before they arise.
- Competition team handbook – guide to your rules at a competition.

Summary

This may be a lot to take in, but I cannot stress enough the importance of getting this right from the start. Then set yourself a review for when you need to check it all, I would suggest annually. I am not a lawyer, I would hazard a guess that most people reading this book are not, but in a court of law, ignorance is not a defence. If in doubt, seek professional guidance.

No matter the situation, never let your emotions overpower your intelligence.

– Unknown

Chapter 9

LOCATION

Location

As the saying goes, 'location, location, location', and there are massive factors associated with this that will dictate where you set up.

- *Where are you living?* In an ideal situation you do not want to be travelling a long way to your venue.
- *Is there a large enough demographic?* If you live in a highly rural area then you may need to consider heading to the most densely populated area.
- *Are there other dance schools in the area?* There is always likely to be competition on your doorstep, but when you set up, you need to give yourself the best possible start. That means staying away from other similar schools, especially in a rural area. Think about the demographic. If it's a city you can afford to have more than one dance school in a small area, but ultimately the area can become saturated. There is only a certain number of people who will want to dance in any given area. Plus, there is an un-spoken rule that demands that respect for other dance schools area and pupils should be maintained.
- If leasing/buying a building, you will be restricted by what is available in your area at the time of looking – please make sure you do your maths! And patience is often the key – if there is nothing available to lease/buy then consider renting for the first years.

The difference between hire or rent, lease or purchasing a building – let's look at the pros and cons…

PROS

HIRE SPACE	LEASE SPACE
Space is ready to use	The building is yours any time of day or night
They pay rates, electric, heat	Do not have to stick to someone else's timetable
Centre will have its own music licence	Do not have to spend hours ringing round halls to find availability on extra rehearsals
Staff on hand to open + close	Can set up all bills by Direct Debit
They will do pat testing, fire alarm testing and Building health and safety regulations	Can decorate anyway you want, including adding a promotional, merchandise and waiting area
Can walk in and start teaching	Can gain additional income through vending machines and letting to other users
They are responsible for the upkeep of the building	

CON'S

HIRE SPACE	LEASE SPACE
Have to stand by their availability	Will need to provide own flooring, bars, mirrors
Need to spend hours ringing around for extra hours	You are responsible for all bills
They can make mistakes and double book	You will need to buy all your own equipment
They will close certain times of the year	You will need to be available to open and close

HIRE SPACE	LEASE SPACE
Have to deal with their invoices (or lack of them)	You will need to do pat testing, fire alarm testing and building health and safety regulations
Often not allowed to use additional space such as meeting rooms or kitchens without prior consent and payment	May need to go early to put on heating
If you have promotional or merchandise you will need to carry to each venue and set up	Deal with opening/closing, invoicing and chasing payments on any other users

This is not a fully comprehensive list but as you can see there are many pros and cons to hire or lease. It needs to come down to what you are comfortable with. In the first instance, while you establish your school, I would certainly recommend hiring because then you are not tied into a long lease contract; and if things not work out then you are able to walk away.

Types of venues to hire:

- Church hall
- Community centre
- Leisure centre
- Another dance school's studio
- College
- Local school
- Theatre studio
- Hotel studio
- Studio of a gym

The most expensive are likely to be council-run centres such as leisure centres and some community centres, and the places that have actual dance studios such as gyms, colleges or other dance schools. The local church hall or community centre will be cheaper, but will not necessarily have the correct flooring, bars or mirrors. So it needs to be an informed decision – what are you willing to sacrifice for a cheaper venue?

Something to bear in mind is that some of the bigger venues would also support you in marketing and promotion, but this is something that you need to discuss with the manager of the centre.

Things to remember when hiring:

Agreements: Whatever type of centre you use, they will always (or should always) use some sort of rental agreement. This will include things like:

Contracts: Your agreement should state what is acceptable and what's not; it's unlikely to include dates and other rentals. Now, this is a consideration; some halls will only rent to one dance studio to avoid a conflict of interest, other halls will rent to whoever they can get money off. Therefore, it's worth having a conversation with the owner/manager to see where they stand on this subject. Then include it in your contract.

Floor: To tap or not to tap, that is the question! Some halls are very particular about whether you can tap or not, because of the marks left. They can also be particular about resin!

Case Study

With one hall I hired, I had three phone calls over three weekends for the following reasons:

Reason 1 – There were four crumbs in the kitchen and we had not hired the kitchen (one of the kids had unwrapped a sandwich on the counter)

Reason 2 – There was one scuff mark on the floor! Seriously! We had to check the floor and potentially clean before leaving.

Reason 3 – The teacher of the next class in complained when she arrived half an hour early, and found my teacher parked in her space, even though the car park is public use!

These are all actual complaints I received from the manager. Sometimes you just cannot judge someone. He had taken me round the building, shown the fire exit, how to lock and so on, and seemed so relaxed about everything, but the truth was he was far from relaxed!

Preparation is the real key here, so get your contracts with your venues in place as this will solve potential problems further down the line.

Footage: Simple question: is it big enough?

Portable bars and mirrors: There are a variety of companies out there that sell portable bars, and you can get bags for ease of carrying too. Portable mirrors are less portable than their name implies. Portable mirrors tend to be moveable rather than portable, so you may need to get permission from the venue to store these.

Yearly contract: This one I find very useful, particularly if you end up using one venue for all of your classes. You could arrange a yearly contract, so that you agree that 52 weeks of the year you are the sole user for either certain days or all week. This means that regardless of whether you use it or not, you pay. This crosses over into leasing but can apply to rental.

Case Study

My competition teams' rentals were proving challenging because of all the constant changes in times due to extras and competitions. Therefore, I was spending many hours a week on finding or cancelling halls and then when the invoices arrived, they were a nightmare to confirm and sort. My answer: I found a hall and hired the space for 52 weeks of the year on a Sunday. Therefore no one else uses it, it's mine between the hours per-arranged and it's mine whether I use it or not. I am not responsible for the building, bills or anything in connection to it, but I am a key holder.

The joy of this situation is that I don't have to spend hours searching for a hall and correcting invoices. The downside is that I still have to pay for the eight weeks a year that I don't use it, but often those eight weeks are either taken by other extra rehearsals or other teams. So it's a win-win for me.

Case Study

A colleague of mine found a church hall to run her dance school; she uses it four days a week, and she has her contract with them outlining that she is the sole user during this time. They have allowed her to decorate and install her own mirrors and bars. The other nights they still rent it out to Weight Watchers and so on. She pays them monthly on direct debit, so she doesn't have to deal with invoices and booking separate hours and so on.

Anything is possible with halls, but you need to find the right venue, in the right location with the right agreement – and get it in writing.

BUYING YOUR OWN STUDIO

OK, so here we go:

Let's just take a moment to understand the undertaking of buying your own studio – as just like any purchase of a house, building and so on there is an associated risk, and there can also be high rewards. Please take professional advice before going to some random auction and bidding on an old church. It really isn't as simple as that

1: You would need a commercial mortgage which would require you to put down a deposit of 25% of the building costs.

2: If buying at auction you only have 28 days to ensure the full funds are in the buyers' bank, which in terms of a mortgage means you may not be able to get one, which then means it's a cash buy.

3: You will need to make sure all the correct surveys and checks have been done.

4: Will you be able to change of use for the building should it require it?

The list goes on and on...My advice is to take advice from the people in the know! Go and see a commercial mortgage advisor well before you start looking for a building. That way you understand how much deposit you are likely to need and can start saving and making allowances.

The list of further requirements continues:

- Interior and exterior design
- Permits
- Licenses
- Health and safety

- Risk assessment
- Music licenses – PPL and PRS
- Air conditioning / heating
- Barres
- Mirrors
- Flooring
- Rates
- Electric
- Water
- Rubbish
- Cleaning
- Security
- Fire Exits
- Signs
- Door closures
- Changing rooms
- Bathrooms
- Pat testing
- Music equipment

The list goes on and on…

It all seems like doom and gloom – but there are massive pros too!

The cost to set up would probably pay you back in a number of years; once you have bought a lot of what is mentioned above, most of it will stay with you for a long time with no need to replace regularly. You will need to do an in-depth budget to understand all your break-evens and profit margins, but even a basic breakdown would probably show you, that if you are renting a space five days a week that you would be better off in the long term with your own place.

Of course there are other benefits – such as being able to generate a further revenue stream by renting out the space. You could start new daytime classes or rent to a daycare centre in the day to generate an extra income. Maybe you could get another colleague who does something different to you, like a performing arts school if you are only dance; they could be an artist-in-residence giving you a steady monthly income.

Your own space would also give the opportunity for a permanent base for your merchandise or a shop for dance wear.

A café is also a possibility. Remember that you don't have to run all of these; the space could be leased from you, because ultimately you don't want to be spending your days making cappuccinos, (unless you want to!). Another option is vending machines – again these can be leased, and in return you get a percentage of the profits.

You could also have your own office, or even rent office space to other artists – maybe a rent-a-day desk?

Think out-of-the-box with a music room, the bonus of this is that it doesn't have to be big, as long as it fits a piano – singing and music teachers are often looking for rooms as they don't all like to teach from their home.

So there are numerous revenue streams you can add to your list of incomes when you come to do the budget for the building. But the biggest pro is the freedom that having your own building brings. There's no ringing around sourcing space for extra rehearsals or exam bookings. No double bookings or having to deal with no-one showing up to open up for you. No incorrect invoices or grumpy caretakers. Freedom to open and close when you want, freedom to spend the day prepping in your studio without having to answer to anyone or technically pay for the space.

Having your own studio is a dream I think all dance school owners have. It's a dream many of us attain to, but it's also a dream that we sometimes choose not to chase. Buying a studio then opening your dance school is probably not the best policy, as an established dance school going into a new building would bring its own regular income. Building the two together would be exceptionally challenging.

As this book is about opening your own dance school, my presumptions are that you are new to this dance school thing. Therefore, I won't dwell on the buying your studio issue. When the time is right, take the right advice, spend a lot of time doing your maths and then make an informed decision.

Summary

Whichever decision you decide to go with, and very likely it is going to be rental in the first instance, then make sure you spend time on the contract, get to know who you are renting from and develop a relationship with them. It will take time and if it is part of a bigger organisation like a council then sometimes decisions are forced upon you, but work your way through them. I should add 'negotiator' onto the dance school owner's job description!

Location is the key to most businesses, and the entrepreneurs typically build their reputation at a particular spot.

– Phyllis Schlafly

Chapter 10

STAFF

Staff

And so... in a land of creatives sits a Dance School Owner with business growth on his or her mind – their only option is to step up (pun intended!) and become the leader they were born to be...

BUT

Before that they have to find some help!

Where do you find them? At the beginning, as you build your studio, a lot of the teaching is likely to be done by you. This not only keeps costs down but it also means that you are building a rapport with those students from the outset. It also means that you're getting to know first-hand what is working within the running of your school and what isn't, and that way you can tweak things as you go along.

If you feel you need to hire staff there are two ways of going about it. You can use a self-employed/freelance person or an employed person. It really depends on what you are looking for because a number of things can be outsourced, and all of these things I will talk about in the next chapter.

Before you take on people you need to do these steps!

Step 1

MATHS! – Have you done the new breakeven points on the classes you anticipate needing a teacher for? Ideally you have the numbers to recruit a teacher and still make a profit. Sometimes it has to work in the opposite way – you may be so busy teaching that you have no time to market the classes – it is at that point that you ned to step back and become a CEO. Take the hit on the class for a period of time to free up your hours so that you can work ON the business, and not IN the business.

Stepping back and driving the marketing and children into the classes whilst someone else does the physical work is an investment into your business AND is the first step to making it grow. BUT word of caution here – set a time limit. DO NOT let that class eat away at the profitability of your other classes for an indefinite period of time. If it takes three to six months can you cope with that hit to profit whilst you drive numbers?

Do the maths!

Step 2

IDENTIFY! – What is it you need help with? Is it a specific style of class that you struggle to deliver or don't like to deliver or something that you do not have the skill set for? Is it admin support? In an ideal world people would like more than one hour in a row of teaching – but if that is all you have, then so be it. What can you give/want /need?

Step 3

BE SPECIFIC! – It is not just a job title. 'Dance teacher required' No – this is your chance to set the scene for WHAT your dance school is about. Retention is all about a happy school – and happy school NEEDS team players. Sometimes you may be desperate and just cannot find someone and then you 'opt' for the wrong kind of person for you school.

'A bad apple will rot the lot!'

A bad apple can have such a negative effect on your school; it can literally SUCK the heart out of it. So be SPECIFIC! Don't settle for second best. You may need to take someone with less experience BUT has the correct 'fit' over someone who has loads of experience but does NOT play by your rules. You can train and give the experience to the person that doesn't have it – but can you teach old dog new tricks?

So when you put your job description out there, BE SPECIFIC!

Not only in skill level, training and standard requirements (DBS, Insurance etc.) but also the qualities you are looking for.

What is it specifically you are looking for? The more detail you can get out there the more likely you are to attract the right kind of teachers/staff to your school.

Are you looking for a highly skilled, technique-driven experienced teacher who can work with senior and advanced only. Who has a passion for excellence and precision, who can teach audition techniques and take the students to the next level?

Are you looking for a bubbly, reliable person who excels at working with preschool age? Who is flexible to jump to other ages, and can commit to weekend and evening work?

If you feel you need to outsource some of the administration work – then please take some advice from someone who has been there, got the t-shirt as well as the matching handbag and shoes... Do not use mums! As much as you might think it would be great as it would save money, perhaps you might even think you could give a class in return for the help – please don't do it! Cardinal Rule number one; never mix mums and business. I cannot stress this enough because it could cause so much grief in the future. For administration work, front desk, or helping with costumes on an adhoc basis ask a friend (not connected to the dance school) if money is tight. Alternatively you could hire someone from a temp agency.

If you need administration work on a regular basis then it would be worth looking to outsource some of it to a VA (virtual assistant). At the beginning, I was dubious because I was reluctant to pay someone to do what I thought I could do myself. Well. Newsflash and humility moment; we're human and sometimes we simply cannot do it all. What a VA can do in one hour could well take us three – so it's money well spent.

Activities you could outsource to a VA:

- Database entries
- Updating email marketing segments
- Website updating
- Bookkeeping
- Managing email
- Social media entries
- Research
- Creating Facebook /twitter / Instagram pages
- SEO (search engine optimisation)
- Entries into online marketing websites
- Designing logos
- Designing memes
- Cutting music

Other means of outsourcing include:

- People per Hour
- Fiverr
- ODesk
- Freelancer
- Elance
- Rev

These sites, a little bit like the VA list above, can do specific jobs that you may not have time for or cannot do. I have used people per hour for a design job on my show planner, Fiverr I have used for memes, and Rev I have used for my new favourite tool in the world, which is to transcribe.

Other examples of outsourcing within the dance school would be:

- Costume manager (done this)
- Head Chaperone (done this)
- Chaperone Manager (done this)
- Music edits (done this)
- Competition Manager (done this)

Some of these people will jump in and out, as roles are temporary but during that period their help is invaluable!

Teaching staff

Most teaching staff are hired on a self-employment/freelance basis. They are responsible for their own tax and national insurance and can work for a number of different people simultaneously. I am not a tax or employment specialist, so you will need to seek professional confirmation, but if a dance teacher is solely working for your dance school then they should technically be employed. Therefore, to avoid you becoming an employer they will need to work for numerous people. So, although it can be sometimes seen as a conflict of interest for your staff to be working in other dance schools, the nature of being freelance means that they are free to work wherever they want.

The positives and negatives of using freelance staff:

POSITIVES	NEGATIVES
Hired on a termly/monthly contract	Can leave with short notice
Can choose not to re-hire if that member of staff is not 'doing their job'	Can work for a competitor
Can add in extra hours or take away easily	Can let you down easily

Life for everyone is easier to manage with a regular wage; therefore, freelance staff are more likely to want regular hours on a weekly/monthly basis. So, although freelance means they can work anywhere, if you get the right member of staff and treat them well, they are likely to stay with you for years.

Hiring

Finding the right teacher for your school is imperative. – they are the backbone of the school, the make or break factor. Get the wrong teacher and you could easily lose a large number of pupils. By the same token, get it right and they will help you grow substantially. In more rural areas it's always going to be more difficult to find talented staff and if they have to travel a long distance to teach then giving them multiple hours will be much more beneficial to them and a more enticing proposition.

When hiring you will need to do a number of things:

1. Advertise the post, giving specifics of styles, days and times (payment at this point does not need to be declared unless you want to);
2. Ask for CVs and references;
3. Shortlist from your CVs;
4. Invite selected candidates for an informal interview, part of which will include a 15-minute teaching slot within a class;

5. Follow up on references;
6. Check DBS certificates/qualifications;
7. Hire, (and give contract).

You can never tell what a teacher will be like until they get in front of a class. I once had a teacher apply who sounded amazing in her interview but when she was in front of a class, I realised she couldn't even hear the beat of the music! You must make sure you check references and are happy with that person's teaching style – remember these teachers are the backbone of the school!

You must check references, qualifications if they are with a board or association, and ensure they have a DBS certificate. If they are freelancing they should have their own music license, stereo and insurance. All of these need to be checked and confirmed, if they do not have their own stereo and you do not have your own base then this is something that you may need to provide. Remember that when hiring freelance staff you will also need to add them to your employer's liability insurance.

All staff should be issued with a contract and new staff should also receive copies of the schools policies. It would be worth adding (although not essential) copies of your school rules, and your expectations of what you expect a teacher to do/act. Within that document you will also need to add in what happens if you get a complaint about the teacher, explaining how as an owner you plan on dealing with that complaint.

In giving the teacher all this paperwork and getting them to sign in agreement of it, they are agreeing to and obeying your rules and regulations.

Perhaps you may be thinking 'Aaargh! This is a bit serious and is it really necessary?' Particularly if you do a community class and there is no real syllabus to follow and so on... But think again, because it is all really necessary! Of course you don't want to stem the flow of the person's creativity or the inspiration that they can bring to the class, however they are working for *you*. This is *your* school and when it goes wrong it is *you* who has to deal with it. If all your staff are on the 'same page' in understanding your expectations of them then it is less likely to go wrong; because then you working as a team towards the same goals.

Payment for your freelancers is decided between the two of you, or maybe you have a school policy on this. Most freelancers are paid either monthly or weekly in arrears. If you are hiring on a project basis, then it is industry standard to pay on completion of the project.

Teacher training

Good leadership is one of the key factors to retaining your staff once you have found them. Communicate, support them, listen to their ideas and contributions and make them feel like a valued member of your team.

As they are self-employed you don't have to pay for them to go on continued professional development (CPD) but ultimately the better their skills are the better your classes and the higher your pupil retention would be. So it's worth considering contributing to their further education. As a rule, you should also be looking to continue your education – not only in dance but also in business. In the shop area of my website www.thedanceden.co.uk you will find numerous classes on finding your ideal client, marketing, mind-set, retention – all great starting points for increasing your business knowledge.

Summary

In addition to this chapter of the book, I would add: be a BOSS! When people start working for you, they are being paid to do a job, and if they are not doing it to standard in a way that ties in with your vision and purpose for the dance school, then they need to be pulled up! Be careful here though, and look at it without blinkers on. Are they not doing it because they are not properly trained or are they not doing it because they are the wrong fit for you and your school? Be a boss, stand up and be strong – it's your school and your reputation.

Train your staff to be always helpful and courteous and knowledgeable. Most importantly, give every member of your staff enough information and power to make those small customer-pleasing decisions, so he never has to say, "I don't know, but so-and-so will be back at..."

– Susan Ward

Chapter 11

EQUIPMENT

Equipment, Apps and Time Saving Technology

These are some of the things you are likely to need and some apps that may prove useful as well. On a plus...they can also save you time, help with marketing and organisation.

OFFICE

- Computer
- Printer

Systems/Apps:

- **Database** – there are numerous options out there – Membermeister (as a member of The Dance Den you get 10% off), Jack Rabbit, Dance Studio Pro, Dance Biz,,,

  I am often asked if it is worth getting a database early into the opening of the school, and my answer is YES! It will save you *so* much time and parents get used to the online element, invoicing and ease of communication.

- **Evernote** – A fantastic app for recording notes.
- **Google Drive** – Cloud storage that I love!
- **Google Docs** – Got to love Google! With this you can create an online enrolment form and then via excel transfer it to your database. It will also transcribe and save you hours typing letters!
- **Mailchimp** – A free (up to 2000 subscribers) e-marketing system. Newsletters, information, segmented customers its fab! Plus they have an offline version for collecting emails at locations where there is no Wi-Fi!
- **iMovie** – (or its android equivalent) we have a visual art form so make your marketing visual too!

Classes:

- **Music System** – You need a music system to play on – it needs high volume, so don't go thinking that the small speakers in your bedroom are going to work in a large dance studio because the sound won't carry. You need to invest in a decent sound system and this usually costs around £150-£250. I currently use a Bosch portable. It fits in a rucksack and has great sound. You will need your phone, computer, iPad or iPod to play the music, and bear in mind that you may also need a jack lead. There are so many portable, loud, Bluetooth systems out there – take your pick!
- **Spotify** – Music streaming service, it is worth paying the extra to get the download for secure piece of mind that you have music to play in class!
- **Back up** – that said – ALWAYS have a backup! My trusty IPod is always charged!
- **Chargers** – Having your phone battery die when you have a child not picked up, is not good!
- **Props** – Always helpful, spots (younger ones) Thera bands, yoga blocks, markers, wands, scarves. You may need a small suitcase to have to hand whatever you need.

Marketing:

- **Boomerang** – A quick, couple of seconds' video for social media.
- **Word Swag** – instant memes.
- **Canva** – another design app.

Other:

- **Bank** – yep – get your bank on your phone!
- **Focus keeper** – an app to help you get focused

Summary

As this book is published there will be more or better versions of the things I've recommended. My advice is to try them, look for others and try them too, see what works for you and use it! If it can save you time do it, if it can get you focussed use it! If it doesn't – bin it!

Technology is moving faster than our pirouettes. If it stresses you, go old school and quietly move forward, learning step by step. If you love it – embrace it and all the hours it will save you, until it goes wrong!

The business changes. The technology changes. The team changes. The team members change. The problem isn't change, per se, because change is going to happen; the problem rather is the inability to cope with the change when it comes.

– Kent Beck

Chapter 12

MARKETING ONLINE

Marketing Online

Before we get into marketing I need to stress the importance of the experience. Online is busy! People are busy! You have such a small window to get people's attention; you need to grab it and fast! The percentage of people using online and mobile devices to access information is HUGE and growing.

70% of people make a decision online BEFORE they contact you (@Chrismarr)

70% is a massive number, so not only do you HAVE to have an online presence, it also has to grab attention fast.

When you create an advert/post/website, in fact anything you need to sell the prospective customer the experience they will gain from coming to your dance class.

Hip Hop Class – tells me what it does, but it does not excite you, entice you or even make you want to join. That is what we do – teach hip hop, but that is NOT necessarily what the customer wants to hear (ironically). If I had a pound for every time someone asked me what is hip-hop? Or what is jazz? Or 'she just wants to dance like they do on the telly'... I am not dumbing down the customer – far from it – but they do not speak our language. If a brain surgeon started marketing to me using neuro pathways and names of drugs – I would be lost! We could have brain surgeons as customers, but they may just never have been involved in the world of dance before. All they know is that their daughter wants to go to a class, make some friends, get fit and wants to dance to the music she listens to on you tube.

So now – create an advert from that....

She will learn hip hop BUT what will she experience?

You're creative...you got this! You know what you feel when you dance, and you know the benefits, so sell them that.......

Back to Marketing Online:

Gone are the days of the proverbial yellow brick, The Phone Book that used to arrive on our doorstep. Back then, the only thing that dictated the number of students you got was the size of your advert. Today's multitudinous media platforms can present a marketing minefield and with new platforms arriving on an almost weekly basis, it's easy to feel lost, confused and overwhelmed.

My advice is to go back to the ideal customer segment we talked about in chapter 6, which asked you to think carefully about where your potential students/parents are hanging out. If they aren't on LinkedIn then don't use it – pick and choose your platforms carefully. This is not a competition as to who had the most social media links on their website; this is about quality over quantity. Meaningful and targeted marketing delivers the best outcomes.

One of the key things you need to have is a website – this alone can bring in the majority of your students and it's also the biggest advert for your dance school. On this platform you can demonstrate your knowledge, show off what you do, give stacks of information and you can keep it fresh and updated.

There are two ways of getting a website:

a) Commission a professional web design company

b) Do it yourself

Web Design Company

Do your homework before you go to a designer. Do you know a good designer? Does your chosen company come via a recommendation? Do they have a good reputation? Can you see examples of their previous designs?

Are you able to access funding? In some areas funding is available for a start-up business, (The Princes Trust is a good provider if you are under 25). If you're looking to use technology or develop the online side of your business then you may also be able to source a small funding pot. Funding for these things is getting harder and harder but it is certainly worth having a look to see what is available.

Even if you get a designer to do the visual and back end work for you will still need to write the copy for your website. At this point I implore you to remember *who* you are selling too. Again go back to the Ideal Client (IC) exercise in chapter 6, or if you're still not clear go to the Dance Den website where you will find a class all about finding your IC. Write your website with your customers' experience in mind. It's not just a dance class, it's a fun, high energy, make-an-insane-amount-of-noise tap class.

Research other dance schools websites, have a clear idea in your head what you like on their sites and probably more importantly what you don't like. If you haven't decided on your branding and logo yet, now is the time to nail it, as all your online and offline marketing will need to look the same.

As dance is such a visual thing, one of the key things to selling what your school is about will be a video, this will demonstrate much more effectively than words what you are about; you can get across your personality, you can show how the classes run and the venue which you operate from. For established schools, a small collage of the last show, students entering for their exams; and then the all-important results shot. People like to see how things work and what goes on. It gives a much better feel for you and your dance school than can be portrayed through words.

On your website you need to include:

- Home page;
- About us/school page;

- Classes;
- Timetable;
- News/events (regularly updated);
- Gallery;
- You will also need links to your social media.

Parents' area

This is not a major detail needed in the first steps of setting up your dance school. You can go old school and just use letters as a form of communication, and with the huge reach of Facebook you may not even find this area useful. But you do need to be able to separate out your communication to your current students from your communication with potential new students.

So you will need to either create a closed Facebook group or have a parent's area on your website where you can post all your handbooks, and your crucial show and exam information. New customers do not want to be seeing notices of 'Your fees are due' or 'today is the deadline for costumes'. Plus, you don't want all your competitors getting your hands on your handbooks, so putting them in a secure password protected area means they can't get at them. I find things like show notices, costumes letters, updates on times, calendars even a tips and advice area within the parents' area all helps towards great communication. It's the hub where they can go and access whatever they need, plus when letters are lost (which they always are!) you can direct them there. Better still, think about the environment and go paperless! Email them that a new exam/costume letter has gone into the parent's area and let them do the looking.

There is a big plus to having a parents' area instead of a Facebook closed group and that is the ease in which you can add pages, and besides, the information is always at hand and easy to find. On a Facebook group the posts will ultimately scroll down as more is added and then finding the correct bit of information is a nightmare. Another massive reason I prefer the parents' area over Facebook is that there is no possible chance of a conversation or discussion into whatever the notice is about. So for example, if you were to post about the class needing red leggings, without fail you will get 40 comments saying things like:

'My daughter doesn't have them. Where do I get them?'

'They are £12.99 in X'

'Whaaat! I'm not paying £12.99, can't they have black?'

(No, Facebook Mum, black is not an option, otherwise black would have been written on the costume letter!)

I don't think it's wise to give parents the chance to counteract or undermine your decisions and a Facebook group gives them that chance. I used the red leggings as an example for good practice. So you don't get parents moaning, tell them where they can get them or better still you get them as a bulk buy. Customer convenience is key and as much as you don't want them moaning at you, you also don't want them moaning about you or the fact that you have given them no guidance or idea as to where they get the costume from.

Marketing sites

These sites are basically event/class listings marketing sites. For free or for a small payment you can enter your details, class venue, type of classes, contact details and sometimes even some photos or a video. A lot of sites of this sort are children-based and advertise various classes, not just dance. So when someone is doing a general search for dance classes in your area, the more sites like this that you're on, with links back to your website, the more likely you are to show up on the first page of Google. Now this can be a big job…

TOP TIP

Do a couple of hours where you batch this as a job lot! Once you've written your advertising spiel you can copy and paste the details across all the various sites. It's also worth mentioning here that you keep a note or excel sheet of all the sites you have entered and the passwords you have used to enter the details. That way when you change your venue/day/time or any other detail, you can go back and find the sites easily to make any changes.

The most popular ones are:

CHILDRENS	DANCE
Netmums	Dance Clubs
What's On 4 Kids	DTOL (Dance Teachers Online)
All for Kids	Dance Near You

On top of this, it's also worth making sure that you're listed with the marketing/promotion sites too, such as Google places, Yell, Yelp, Gumtree and Free Index. You may also find that your local council advertises certain events or classes on their website, or maybe that the venue you use offers the possibility of listing your classes online too. Make sure you explore all the possibilities.

There are also marketing sites on social media. LinkedIn, Facebook and twitter all have local groups where you can post and advertise your classes. Remember with social media, posts tend to get long lists of events which are added, so it may be worth asking if your classes can get pinned to the top. Alternatively, you may need to go back in and post a couple of times in the run up to your classes starting.

Social media

Oh where to start! And no doubt by the time this book is published it will be out of date! The fast-paced, ever-changing world of the internet is probably one of the most valuable tools you will need in your marketing toolbox. There are a plethora of social media platforms that you could use to get your message out there, so should you use them all? The simple answer is no. There are way too many for you to manage them all in a constructive and effective manner. As a rule, because social media is a constant turnover of posts, tweets and pictures and the amount of content that is being added by the hour or second is insane, getting your message out there in front of the right people has never been harder. Which is why you should be posting at least three to four times a day on the most appropriate social media platforms.

'Impossible!' I hear you cry! I thought so too when I was first getting my head into marketing. Given that I grew my business the old school way, the learning curve of social media has been a massive eye opener. Even now though I post once a day on Facebook and three to four times a day on Twitter (excluding retweets). This in a social media expert's eye would not be enough – but in actuality it's better than most. And whilst I still have two small children and a third child called the 'dance school' to run, and whilst it is still gaining a good following and reach, then I shall continue at this rate for the moment!

So, back to the various social media platforms, how do you decide which one is best for you? Well, the answer is you don't decide! Simply focus on where your customers hang out because that will dictate which platforms you should be using. Go back to the IC exercise in chapter 5, look at who you are trying to attract and aim your social media at them.

Are they on Facebook? If I should be so bold as to stick my neck out here – yes, of course most of them are. So you need to get on it!

Twitter? Not as much direct business pick-up here, but it does raise the profile.

Instagram? Very popular with the teenagers.

Pinterest / Bing / Google / Flicker / Blogging platforms / Myspace / Vimeo / You tube? What works for me will not necessarily work for the next person. *You* have to find out where *your* customer is hanging out and you need to be in there too.

Facebook

Earlier in the chapter I talked about a closed Facebook group for your parents, and briefly mentioned a page. Let's take a moment to focus on this as a marketing tool for your business. Although the general reach of Facebook is getting worse unless you are paying for ads it's still a good 'shop window' for your business.

TOP TIPS

- Ensure you fill in the 'about' section and make sure there is a hyperlink back to your website

So many people don't fill out this section fully and it's a perfect chance for you to advertise what your school is about.

- Header

This is the picture header at the top of the page, make sure this looks exciting and says what it does on the tin! Remember when you design this that the profile pic and the categories writing goes over the top, so make sure you take this into account. Spell out to your customers what it is you do. The Mary Jones Dance School tells me who you are, but the name of the page and the profile pic should say that anyway. Design this so that it screams 'beautiful ballet in a fun, supportive, qualified environment' or 'urban street styles in a hip, fun packed, friendly studio'. Use every opportunity to say 'what you do' rather than who you are.

You can design your own headers, memes and pictures for your posts for free at Picmonkey or Canva.

- Schedule, schedule and then schedule some more

If my advice for posting three to four times a day made you do a 360 then this is about to become your lifesaver! There is an arrow next to the word 'post' on Facebook, click that and you can schedule your posts to go out when you want. Now, if you want to get technical, then you can look into insights and judge when your customers are most likely to be on Facebook and who the demographic is and so on... but for now, just post! Get your information out there! I love batching so much, because you get a job and then you get it done and then you don't have to do it again!

Imagine only having to post on Facebook 12 times a year! How amazing would that be! Well you can do it – plan out what is happening in your month ahead, so when you have a competition, or when there is a countdown to your new class starting. Plan and then type away and schedule, and then anything else you want to add in the process of the month, you can, but if you forget or you don't get time to do something, then at least something will get out there. Facebook loves regular postings and you are more likely to get your stuff seen by others if you are a regular poster, so get on it.

What can you post? What if you don't think you have enough to say or share?

Here are a few ideas that might help if you're stuck:

- **About you:** lots of people won't know you, or your past training. If you were a professional dancer, share a photo or a story from your travels.
- **Explain your classes:** go into detail on 'what is street' or this is what I do in my stretching class; educate your potential or current customers on the love, care and effort that go into making the classes what they are
- **Memes:** these are funny pictures that people are likely to share (you can make these on Canva or PicMonkey)

- **Tips or how to's:** your students would love these, and it's also a great way to start building a presence on Youtube.
- **Photos:** Of your students (with permission) or stock photos
- **Questions:** ask a question 'who would like to see XYZ dance school have its own water bottle?'
- **Run a competition:** just make sure you abide by Facebook rules.
- **Sales:** Yep, actually post about your spaces in your classes, but don't do this all the time as it will put people off.

Don't use your Facebook page as a sales page, even though it is. Think about it, how would you like to get 'sold' to all the time, I know that I would stop going to that page. People love to hear stories, see videos, photos, share content – so be generous and share your knowledge, show people that you know what you're talking about. This will build trust and people start to like and talk about you, that's the way your reach and your likes will grow.

In this second edition (January 2018), it is worth mentioning that Facebook has just changed its policy/algorithms to bring news feedback to community based interactions. How this will affect business, time will tell. There are many experts out there giving their views on the subject. In my opinion, dance schools are locality based, we are not selling to the masses and a lot of what we do is community based, so a huge percentage of our customers WILL come from word of mouth or recommendation. So will this change affect us as locality based businesses? I don't think it will – as long as your Facebook page is entertaining, informative and not always sales, I don't think we will notice much change…but time will tell!

What Facebook is increasingly pushing businesses towards is Facebook advertising. I am not an expert on this subject…so I cannot give you a cheat's guide to using it. What I do know is this:

- *Target, target and target* – too much money is wasted on wrong targeting.

- *Test, review, repeat* – Test for small amounts, see if it works, make alterations and then repeat the test, tweak until you have one that works!
- *Learn (I am!) and take a course* – there are online ones from Udemy and many others. Read, listen and take in as much information as you can. Make it a challenge, newbie to expert in x months. My den members who are jumping on the challenge are seeing really good results. So Facebook is still an amazing marketing tool, just don't get caught up in spending too much money on the wrong type of advert!

Another great way of demonstrating that you know what you're talking about and acknowledging your expertise in this subject (remember, people need to trust you because they are giving you their daughter/son to teach) is to blog. Is it worth you setting up a blog for your dance school? Is this something that would benefit the school?

OK, we'll get real and look at the positives and negatives, but before we do that, let's be honest! Do you like to write? Because if this is going to become another thing you don't manage on your to do list because you keep putting it off, don't start! The positives outweigh the negatives, but I personally don't have a dance school blog – simply because I have enough to do with my two businesses and if I cannot do it justice and give it my full attention then why would I start it?

It does however have massive positives:

It positions you as an authority on your subject – so that when new clients who know nothing about ballet, for example, read your posts on, how to tie shoes, improving turn out and so on, they'll think 'Oh, she knows what she's talking about' and it starts to build trust, and the more trust you build the better, and the more likely they are to buy from you.

You can gain feedback – by asking a question out there, you responses could guide you on whether you start new classes or not.

Likes and shares are great. If it's a great blog post and it is shared on social media as well as your website then it is more likely to attract a new audience through social media which you can then in turn drive to your website and hopefully from there convert them to clients.

You can re-use the material in your blogs as posts on Facebook and tweets.

Google loves blogs; because it sees your website as having added new content and its search algorithms will always push websites that add new content higher up the rankings than those that don't.

Here are the negatives, though:

- You need a website you can change easily, not one that you need to keep paying a designer to do.
- You need to write!
- You need to publish regularly.

A blog is a great tool if used correctly, but it can also be something that drains your time. So before you start, think hard about what you are trying to achieve, and make sure it's the right thing for you.

Twitter

Before you start tweeting, check how many of your customers are on Twitter. It's a great tool for raising awareness and getting your school into the public eye and even attracting celebrities who could endorse your school. But let's be realistic, if you're just starting out, surely that's not your priority? Your priority would be getting your information in front of mums, and are those mums hanging out on

Twitter? They may have an account but are they really active?

That said, I do have a Twitter account for my business and I am highly active on it and it has helped considerably in raising the profile of the dance school further afield. Yes, I have gained students through it, but you do need to join the Twitterati to achieve results.

TOP TIPS

- As with Facebook, make sure your profile is fully updated and links go through to your website. You can reuse your Facebook header.
- Use hashtags as carefully as possible. If you use 10 in a post it's overkill! Use two or three but make them really specific. #your school #newclass #someone who may share what you have to say. So # in a mums' group, local event and press.
- You can make lists

There are loads of other forums that you can get on – I just need to stress that you need to do your research before you learn and spend time on a platform that will not give you the returns you need for your time investment.

Hootsuite is certainly worth a look as this programme can schedule all your social media posts in one place and automatically send them all out.

Email marketing

The saying is 'the money is in the list', and in most cases, this is very true if you are a product-based company. If you sell gifts for example, offering a 10% money-off voucher for a Valentines special will generate both money and orders. But dance is a service-based industry, so generating those kinds of sales via a list won't have the same effect. However, you should still have one because ultimately your dance classes themselves are a product, so you need to think about them that way.

When you start gathering a working email list of past, possible and new enquiries, they become the first people you can sell to and since they are on your list because they have expressed an interest in buying from you, they are the people who are more likely to buy from you now. Often, someone may enquire, but the timing isn't just right; but if they're on your list, you can keep them informed of the next intake, or a new class starting. If they took the time to enquire in the first place, then they like your school, you need to nurture that, don't let that enquiry slip.

Plus if you have a pop-up shop of merchandise, or have a show, workshop or anything one-off, those enquiries may not be ready for regular classes but they may well give a one-off workshop a go just to test the water. So just because they do not attend your classes, it doesn't mean that they are not or cannot be your customers in another form.

So you need to create a list. If you have a database then, depending on which one you decided to get, it may have an e-marketing facility in it. If so, start with that because if you can keep it all contained then that would be really good. If they don't then it's worth looking at the following programmes:

- **MailChimp** – this is free for up to 2000 subscribers, but there is a paid version too.
- **Aweber** – paid subscription, but very comprehensive.

For starting purposes, MailChimp is great. It is advisable that once you start on one programme you stick to it, because transferring 2000 mailing lists at a later date is a nightmare!

Case Study

I used my own Microsoft email address and created an address book of all enquiries, which worked great up until the point that I had over 1000 email address and then changed phone/ broadband provider. In the changeover, even though it was a business line, there was a limit put on my account as to how many emails I could send per hour in order to avoid spam. The business limit was 50! It took me 20 hours to do a mail out, basically three days! Every hour sending one newsletter! As you can imagine, I probably did two a year because of the sheer effort involved.

So I researched email marketing companies and discovered MailChimp, and my monthly newsletter now takes me half an hour to design and five minutes to send! And now, the newsletter is monthly!

MailChimp and Aweber give you templates with which you can create lovely designs, and you can add links to your website, pictures, change the text and so on. They are both very comprehensive programmes.

But there are a couple of things you need to do so that you do not spam people. When people enquire, give them the choice to be added to the mailing list or not, don't just assume that it will be OK – legally you do need to ask.

When people have subscribed to the list you need to make it easy to unsubscribe – MailChimp does this for you. You will need to make it quite clear that their email address is not passed on to any third party.

Things you can send to your list:

- Monthly newsletter – this is really important and as with your Facebook posts make sure that you add interesting content.
- Notice of a new class/workshop/show
- Notice of a pop-up shop / merchandise sale
- Announcements

Emailing is a great way of communicating in a professional manner, but you will need to create separate groups – past, enquiries, new starts, no shows, and then send emails according to the group they are in to attract, keep or help them. New enquiries are not going to want to know there is a problem with the hall this Saturday, current ones will! So be careful what you send to the entire list.

Summary

I cannot stress enough the importance of choosing what works for you. There are so many platforms out there, that just jumping on bandwagons will burn you out. There are only so many hours in the day, and even with scheduling and automation, these things still have to be set up. Choose what works and run with it.

Marketing is getting someone who has a need to know, like and trust you.

– John Jantsch

Chapter 13

MARKETING OFFLINE

Offline marketing

Public relations (PR)

Have you:

- Ever done a flash mob?
- Freestyling in the town centre?
- Taken a pop-up stall in the town centre?
- Managed to get on your local radio?
- Managed to get yourself on the local TV?

All of this is free publicity, and it takes work to do it or get it, but it's so worth it when you get there. This has a lot to do with your networks and connections – whom do you know who can get you on that radio slot to talk about the benefit of ballet? If you've won a big competition, maybe the local TV will cover it? Could you do a charity flash mob?

Marketing is all about memory – the saying is 'the rule of seven' – people need to see you seven times before they buy – it's the accumulative build-up of trust.

So think about it – maybe they have seen you a couple of times on Facebook with people sharing, liking and posting about the school. Then maybe they see a press article or an advert, or someone walking around wearing your jumper. They've heard a friend talk about it in the school yard – and all of a sudden they are hearing your dance school name, time and time again. So when it comes to choosing a dance school, who are they likely to turn to? You!

Media relations

There's no rhyme or reason to gaining press coverage! You could write the most amazing press release and it still may not get covered. Sometimes it's more to do with timing than anything else. To maximise your chances, what you have to do is find an angle to base your story on – it won't be covered if it looks like advertising. So, find an angle:

- *Human interest* – a child has come back from injury to win a national award.
- *Connect with current events* – e.g. aTV-related angle; dance team awarded XYZ by so and so from TV show.
- *Business and community angle* – tell your story; new entrepreneur brings exciting style of dance to Hampshire or ex-dancer returns from world tour to share her knowledge

Once you have sent your press release, keep in contact, chase the article, and don't assume they will run it, sometimes they need to be reminded. Don't be afraid to call them and say, *Have you received it? What did you think? Do you need more information?*

Newspaper reporters are inundated with information, so yours needs to stand out. Or else they need to drop a story in at the last minute and you happen to call and so yours gets put in. Once you have your contact, keep in touch with them, build a connection with them, ask them what sort of stories your local paper likes to run and then angle your news to what they like to publish.

Leaflets

Many say that leaflets are dead! I disagree – Long Live Leaflets! I still get numerous enquiries from my leaflets. The key is getting them out there and into schools. It takes effort and time, but it's definitely worth it.

Don't overload it – focus your marketing and remember *who* you are trying to attract. If you need more ballet students, have a leaflet for ballet. If you need younger students then will creating a young-looking leaflet catch attention? You're selling an experience, not just a tap class!

TOP TIP

See if your printers can put your leaflets in packs of 30-35 if you're doing a school run. The schools will love you for it, because it makes their job easier, and that means they are more likely to go out than end up in the bin.

Signage

This is so important and it has become a bit of a bugbear of mine, not through choice, but I find the more dance studios I attend the more I seem to find that they hide where they are.

But let's look at this from a number of areas:

- *Hired venue* –It's difficult to put up permanent signage here, but with permission you can still put it up while you are teaching. Not only will this help new trials to find you, but think about the passing trade!
    - Large banners on railings
    - Pop up banners in windows
    - Flags
- *Your own venue* – This is where you can go to town. Make sure you have really strong signage on the front of the building. You can put popups in the windows too, as these can be changed as the marketing rotates. Another top tip is the back of the toilet door....yep! Are you low on numbers in a certain class, or need more adults in your dance fit? Attach something to the back of the door (like they do in the service stations!) Any chance you have to get your information in front of the customer – do it!

Radio

Are there local radio stations where they do what's on events? Do they do guest sections where they get experts in to talk about the latest trend or TV Show? Do they have a business show where you can jump on and talk about your new venture?

There are so many opportunities out there, it is worth asking, it is also worth you introducing yourself so that they are aware you are around and willing to chat.

Summary

If you work the two forms of marketing on- and offline, together, they provide a powerful campaign to get you noticed. Not everyone is attracted to social media, and not everyone is on Facebook... you need to be in multiple forms and in many ways. That way you have a blanket approach to your marketing BUT in a very niche, segmented way.

Don't underestimate the value of someone who is clever with words.

– David Counsell

Chapter 14

ADDITIONAL REVENUE

Additional Revenue

So I have a whopping 25 other income streams that I talk to my members about in The Den but for now we are going to focus on the 'big ones'. I'm quite excited by some of these because they are quite 'out there' and potentially you have never thought about them before. I would recommend though, that you don't count on these extra income streams. If your dance school cannot sustain itself on classes alone, then you need to go back and revisit the maths! Any extras should be seen as 'additional' or as an added extra to the classes. These will help boost it, supplement it, and give you that little bit extra. It shouldn't be the be-all and end-all of everything. What I'm saying is, if you do none of this, you should still be able to make money. So you need to make sure your classes are earning what they need to be earning and are spot on as far as those numbers go.

Merchandise

Now this is all about the bags, the teddy bears, lanyards, keyrings, water bottles and so on. It's the 'things', the 'items'. You can buy a water bottle with your logo on in quantities of 50/100/200 for around £1.50/£2, and then if you then sell for £3.50/£4 that's a 50% mark up on every water bottle you sell. You sell your 50/100 water bottles, you're slowly adding a drip feed into your income. Add that with a bag here, a pen there, some little items as 'impulse buys'. You know when you stand in queues, and you're waiting to be served, and they always have items by the till, something that's on offer etc. The cashier may even say to you 'these are on offer today. Would you like them?' and you just think 'Go on then!' That's an impulse buy, because it was there in your face. If they're not there on display to look at as a potential impulse buy they you won't get that money. Find somewhere where you hire or in your own studio that you can set up a little shop full of impulse buys. All these little things add up!

Uniform

Depending what type of school you are you may have a set uniform for your dancers. For example in ballet you need your hair a certain way, certain shoes etc. I know in this day and age, with the internet squeezing a lot of the profit margins for us on these sorts of items it is getting harder. However nothing, I mean nothing, will ever follow for convenience. People will always pay for convenience. For example, if a mum walks in and says 'My daughter needs a new leotard, please can I have one in size 4?' If you have it there in front of her to hand she can buy immediately she will pay slightly more to have it there and then instead of driving to a dance shop, or searching online and ordering, with no certainty of whether it will fit or not. If the fit is wrong, then she will need to go to the trouble of sending it back and then she's got all the extra postage costs. Customers will pay a little extra to have the convenience of having something instant. We're in the day and age of people wanting things in an instant 24/7, instant answers, instant access; it's getting more and more like that. If you can provide that, so what if you're more expensive than online? If someone does say to you, 'This is cheaper online,' then you can turn around and say 'Go ahead, but if it's the wrong size you'll have to go through all the postage costs and effort of sending it back. However, this is it; you can try it on and if it fits, take it now.' Given that choice, it's almost guaranteed they will say 'OK!' Don't feel like you can't compete with the online sellers, because you're not technically competing with them, you're offering a different service. It is that service, that convenience, that attention to detail and confirmation that people will pay extra for. So yes, you can make money on uniforms. You can also make money on merchandising – T-shirts, leggings, and hoodies all with your logo on! If you are a dance school that doesn't necessarily use leotards, you can still enforce a uniform across the school that involves a t-shirt or hoodie etc. that is not leotard based but has your logo on it. It's a double whammy really, because if they go shopping or somewhere wearing it they are marketing your school and representing it while out in public but also you're earning money off them buying those t-shirts/hoodies.

Tuck shop

If you have your own studio this should be a no-brainer for you specifically. If you have a little waiting area, you can put in a vending machine, a coffee machine and a little tuck shop selling water, fruit and sweets, and it will slowly tick along for you. The only thing you potentially have to do is fill them up. However, there are companies that will do it for you, and give you a percentage of the profits. So there are a couple of options here where you don't need to do the work and you can take a smaller percentage of the profits, or you can do the work and buy a small fridge and stock it with whatever you need and take a bigger percentage of the profits. There is another way of doing it if you rent your property: take it with you. Set up a table with an honesty box, price everything up and people just buy and put money in the box. You don't need to man it; on the whole people are trustworthy and will pay their dues. Especially when you have children buying things, parents like to teach them the right thing. They're not going to say 'Yeah just take it and don't bother paying,' as that's not the right thing to demonstrate to the child. When it comes to filling it, you can go to trade suppliers that supply all the corner shops etc. and you can become a trade customer because you are a business. You can do 'B2B' which is business to business, you can go to these trade warehouses e.g. Bookers, Costco. Go to these warehouses and buy in bulk, store them and drop into the tuck shop when needed. We have one at my dance school but I don't run it. We use this as a fundraiser for the competition team and it's those mums that run it. They bring it, they stock it, they go, and I have to say they've had a steady earning from it. One of the venues I use is a big leisure centre and because of the footfall going by, they have been known to make £40 a night. Another way of buying is offers in main supermarkets; they'll often do offers of big boxes of crisps for £4 or £5, which then works out cheaper than the warehouse! So it's worth keeping an eye out for those sorts of deals, as it's a steady income from a tiny bit of work. You don't have to sell at a ridiculous price; you'll still be making 50/60% profit on each item, that's a really good return.

Exams

Why are these in here when it may be part and parcel of your dance school? This goes back to what I said at the beginning about your regular classes. This is what really needs to earn your grass roots level, you should be making money off this, and then everything else is the cream of the crop. And your exams are the cream of the crop. Now, exams are expensive, yes. And they're expensive for you guys as well, by the time you get the examiner down, and they need certain things and the room has to look a certain way, following a strict protocol. So yes, it can be more expensive for you to run an exam, so I'm not saying necessarily you will make money from the exam itself but where you *will* make money is the lead up to the exam itself. It'll be the new leotard, the new tights, the new shoes, the private classes, the specific exam preparation class, the lesson to the parents to make sure the hair is right, even the practice run. It would be all of those things in lead-up that you will need to charge for that will be extra. These things are where you will make your money, if not necessarily the exam itself. You might want to add an admin fee on the exam. If the board is charging you £50 a head, you might want to make it £70 – that's your choice for you to earn a little extra. I don't see a problem in adding an admin fee to the exam due to the sheer amount of work that's involved in putting students in for an exam. You may think it's not a bad idea! There's lots of ways for you to make little bit more income surrounding exams.

Dance Parties

Remember if you start doing dance parties, they are a big commitment, particularly on evenings and weekends. It's a good income earner and dance parties are a great way of moving forward, because not only will it promote your school but it's a nice little earner for a couple of hours work. But the commitment here is huge so bear that in mind before you launch your dance parties. Do you really want to spend your Saturdays and Sundays doing dance parties? If you do decide to do them, do you say, 'Right, I will only do X amount a month,' or 'I will only do Sundays'? There are ways of organising your time so you can decide what you do on your terms, and I really want you to keep that in mind before you launch dance parties. The other thing to remember is you can always add an additional income on by providing party bags. You can make a little bit of money by providing little things like a fancy dress costumes etc. There's an option to make a little bit more money there as well.

Wedding dance

Now this is a lovely one! If you think about weddings, people always whack up the price. But having a very specific dance tailored to your clients takes some skill, which you've all got, and it would be lovely to deliver this special moment for this couple. But not everyone will want a traditional wedding dance; others may want a more modern one. So don't feel that if your skills are more street dance-based that this will not apply to you, because it might well do. Maybe you're that specialist wedding dance person that people will go to for something out of the ordinary, and that's a great niche to move into. You can also think about how maybe, if you are that more niche person, you could reach out to a ballroom person and, say, if a traditional one comes in, ask them to do it for you. Then, if you're charging say £50 for every session, or whatever you decide your figure is, and then you subcontract that client to this person, they'll still be earning £30/40 an hour and you are still making a small profit. That's a nice little added on income earner for you!

Costumes

This is always a difficult one because there's always the feeling that you don't want to fleece your customers, and I feel quite strongly on that, because if your customers think 'Oh no, more money for this again,' they may feel it's just too expensive, and they may leave. You need to get the balance right, but ultimately costumes take an awful lot of work to source, to fit, to find, to return, to alter etc. There's so much involved in it that it just doesn't make sense to me that you can't make money from it. If you're giving it to them for cost price then in effect you are losing money because of all that extra time that's involved. Then you're not taking your break-evens properly into account because you're not taking into account the hours spent sourcing: when the box arrives, you double check it to make sure it's all there and all right. This is all your time and time is money. You need to make sure you're making money from your costumes. It's also a question of value or perception, that when you buy in a costume what do people perceive that value to be? You may actually find you perceive the value to be lower that the customers do. Bear this in mind: you should really be making money from costumes. If you have a street school or with street classes like me and you're buying things from a sports shop or Primark etc. they have the tag on them so people can obviously see the price you paid for them. Why not add an admin fee? That then covers your parking, your time, your transport, and people won't mind paying admin fee. If you charge a £5 admin fee and you have 200 students, that's £1000. That money will then contribute to the postage costs, the returns. You'd be surprised, I can spend at least £40 on parking when it comes to show time and if you hadn't charged an admin fee for those costumes you would be out of pocket £40.

Extra Rehearsals

In the lead up to festivals, competitions, exams and shows specifically, there is always going to be a need for extra rehearsals. If you put a big finale together, you'll need a finale rehearsal, a dress rehearsal, and a tech rehearsal. These all need to be charged for and are in addition to your regular classes and therefore are a supplementary income.

Workshops

There are two ways of looking at this. You can put on a workshop using the teachers you already have or yourself, and you would use it as a skill-specific workshop. i.e. you could do a stretching intensive, a turning intensive or if there is something you have gone away and learnt, such as a new skill in hip-hop, then you bring it back and do a specific one-off workshop based on that. It's all in-house, it's all from you and it's a one-off or, say, three times a year. This is separate from your regular classes and therefore, because it is a specific skilled class, you can add it on as an extra. Another way of looking at this is bringing in an outside professional to workshop maybe a skill you don't have, or maybe a visiting performer who has danced for Beyoncé and is doing a masterclass for your school. It's a good retention policy, and it is a good earner for you at the same time.

Short Course

This is very much along the idea of a workshop, but this is an expanded workshop in effect. So you do a six-week spin class, a trick class, a strengthening and flexibility class, a specific waaking class etc. Whatever it is, you sell it in bulk and in advance. People book onto it for the full six weeks, it is in addition to your regular classes and it helps with retention and helps with your bottom line.

Summer School/Summer Camp

This is a lovely way to earn extra income as long as you get the numbers in. If it's a regular thing for you, then you're probably well established, and if there isn't much competition around you it'll probably be really good for you to set up something like this! Do a week and the children come all day. Parents that work the 9-5 jobs do struggle to find things for their children to do and they're looking for activities. Make sure you sort it out well in advance; get your marketing out there. I have known clients who have sold their summer schools in April and they are full. What can you do that is different to what is out there? Maybe no schools around you offer it. Think about what you want to do with timings and schedules etc. If you're bringing in new people to your dance school and they like it, they may stay and become customers. So again, it's another way of bringing new people into your school.

Shows

Shows are fantastic ways of earning an income as long as you get your maths right from the outset. If you are a musical theatre school, your costs may be much greater than a dance school. This is because of performance rights, an orchestra, a much larger set than a dance school, and so your costs are going to be that much higher. How many pupils do you have? How many tickets are likely to be sold? Do you need a smaller venue? Don't go to a 2000 seat venue if you're just starting out. I don't anticipate you would, because I presume it would be fairly common sense to start small and build up. You've got to take into account technicians' costs – are they included or separate? What about ticket costs – are you selling tickets? Or does the theatre sell them? if they do, they're likely to take a percentage at box office. You've got things like programmes where you can do advertisings and potentially make money off as well. If you put enough bums on seats to coin the phrase, then yes potentially at the end of it you will make money for yourself. But it is a tall order, it's a big ask and does take a lot of work! I can't see why you wouldn't earn money at the end, but it's always a bit of a risk because it's a high cost item and you don't know where you stand with your figures until all the seats are sold and the show has finished – only then will you know your actual numbers. So really, if you're doing a show you've got to keep an eye on your budget and costs and make sure it doesn't run away with you. It's very easy for it to run away with you, what is your breakeven point? If you're not hitting your breakeven point what can you do to ensure you hit that?

In The Dance Den I have developed a show planner that is a one stop guide for your shows, everything from budgets, marketing, costumes, lightings – it's all in there. Check out www.thedanceden.co.uk.

You could also offer:

- Competition classes
- Private classes
- Adult classes

Additional income revenue streams

- Photography + videography
- Online programmes

Summary

Please do not rely on these things as your break-even; this is most defiantly the cherry on the top. Some of these will take time to set up and maybe a few years down the line, some may not work with your school, but pick and choose. Get your maths right and you can add greatly to your bottom line.

Work hard in silence. Let your success be your noise.

– Frank Ocean

AFTER YOU OPEN

Chapter 15

LAUNCH DAY

Launch day

When opening a new school it's a wonderful marketing opportunity to do a countdown to launch night. There are widgets and apps online that you can add to your website to show an actual countdown in days, hours and minutes. Given that you haven't actually taught a class yet it will be very difficult to gain testimonials, videos and pictures of your school, all of the essential things you need for your website and for marketing to demonstrate in the lead up to launch what you are about. So there are a couple of things you can do to accommodate this.

Firstly, if you have taught as a freelance teacher in other schools or community classes, is there a way you can get any testimonials or photos from them? Do not assume your previous boss will be OK with this; you will need to ask and gain permission first. Your video could just be you talking about the ethos of what you stand for, qualifications and so on; maybe you can borrow a child or a few children and demonstrate a few exercises.

A really good way to build momentum in the lead up to launch day is to hold an open day. 'But I don't have anything to show!' I hear you cry. But really, you have everything you need. Advertise an open day where people can get a free class/demonstration and meet the teacher(s). Here are a few ideas of what you can offer/do to make it more exciting:

- Hire the hall you will be using and advertise the demonstration time, or numerous demonstrations of the different styles.
- Put up banners outside and pop-up banners inside.
- Balloons, tablecloths, bunting and any promotional material make the hall look nice.
- Have a table or rail of your uniform and shoes they will need. You will need to have this stall manned by someone; people will have a lot of questions about necessity and cost.

- Have a hair demonstration; yes there are people out there who cannot do a bun! (Me included!)
- Have friends or family on hand to do a meet and greet and direct people to you.
- Make sure you are wearing a T-shirt or something that says who you are; people will want to talk to you.
- Have a selfie station, or a hashtag post, so people can be active in social media.
- Get local press involved.
- Hire a local mascot, celebrity or even a dress up character to add to the entertainment.
- Make sure all your helpers are fully aware of your prices, class times, what you do; you need to brief them beforehand.
- Give all who attend a bring-a-friend card, with an offer.
- Give visitors the opportunity to enrol on the open day night.
- Have a free cup of tea and cake stall.
- Have a balloon for all the children who attend, make sure it has your logo and brand all over it!
- Have one person dedicated to gathering email addresses or phone numbers, so if they're not sure you can call them after the event to thank them and ask them if they need any further information.

Open days are an amazing way of gathering interest and excitement around the new school, but make sure that you have heavily advertised the event; there is nothing worse than a poorly attended event for putting people off. I cannot stress enough the importance of briefing everyone who is helping your event. They need to know:

- What you are trying to achieve from the open day;
- All class times, days, venues, costs;

- What the uniform is and how much it costs;
- How people can enrol;
- What happens after enrolment;
- If you do exams, shows and competitions;
- How people can pay;
- If there is a trial lesson/period.

Your staff need to be fully informed, so they can answer all questions, because it will reflect badly on you if they can't answer the questions. Think about how annoying it is if you go into a shop and the assistant can't answer your queries and goes off to find the manager, and five minutes later you're still waiting. It screams 'unprofessional' and that you don't know what you are doing, and with a new school this is your key chance to impress.

The same formula can be used for 'open days' when you are established. With this you can add in demonstrations, solos, or a sample class and you can get your dancers walking around in costumes. A beautiful tutu always attracts attention.

Summary

A really well-organised day can be a massive benefit to your school from many angles. You can raise awareness about your school, you can sign on new pupils, and you can create new opportunities and connect with people who come to see your day. Most important are the sign-ups, the uniform sales and those email addresses, so make sure you follow those up!

The greatest amount of wasted time is the time not getting started.

– Dawson Trotman

Chapter 16

ENROLMENT

Enrolment

The enrolment process is going to be a very personal thing. We all run our schools differently, and everyone has their way. When you can systemise or process your enrolment, it stops potential customers slipping through the cracks.

Think of it this way: when someone emails, you need to send them on a path, a journey to get them into your school. If you actually did the maths on how many pupils you lost because they didn't show up for their trial lessons, I think it would be actually quite high if you're doing the whole 'Yeah, yeah, just come along on Friday' -type booking system.

Whereas, when you get a much more detailed and much more consistent process in place, two things happen.

The first is that they're more inclined to turn up to the trial class because it's a specific booking in place. Just even that word, 'booking', will help them or even force them to come along. The second is simply that, when eventually you want to maybe pass this on to an admin person, the process is tried, tested and works. There is a system, and all you have to do is train them up on it so they can take it over.

A good system for you to develop whilst working out your enrolment is the Three Cs, Clarity, Consistency and Conviction.

- **Clarity** – There needs to be clarity of the process, of the pathway, of the journey, clarity that's going to know that once this step is done, you go on to step two and then on to step three and the clarity just goes right the way through the whole process.
- **Consistency** – There needs to be consistency of every single enrolment that you take, no matter what form it comes from, whether it's from a call, Facebook, email, Instagram or texts.

- **Conviction** – There needs to be that call to action. When people inquire, you have to push for them to say, 'Yes, we will be there.' You have to get them to make that connection and make them turn up so there has to be conviction in what you are doing.

There are two things that you need to create to yourself, to help the enrolment process:

1 – **Have a master sheet of your responses for every single class that you teach.** A standard email that includes all the information that they need to attend that class. When you respond to your emails in the morning, you just open this master sheet up the same time so that you can copy and paste into the email and just change names, or possibly a date. It just saves you so much time. It also means that there is clarity, consistency and a call to action ready made for you, and this way you won't forget anything.

2 – **Have an Excel sheet for tracking**. Create a chart with room for their name, email, telephone number, the child's name, date of birth, parents name, date in, date responded, which class you've sent them a trial for, and any notes. For marketing purposes include a 'how you heard' field and make sure to include a tick box to check whethere they have given permission for e-marketing

Every time you get an inquiry in, you need to fill this, and that way you can track where you are in the process. You don't want people falling through the gaps. By using this form and tightening up the enrolment process, you can stay on top of those inquiries. Then you can daily look back to that Excel sheet and go, 'Hmm, I emailed that person three days ago and they didn't respond. Let me just text them or email or ring them and go, did you get my email?' And then you could follow up from there.

Now there's no template that I can give you for this. I think I'm on version six of my templates now. You will find certain things work for you and certain things don't. You may prefer it on a notepad, on a piece of paper or in the back of a diary or on your phone. For me it works on an Excel sheet. I can see it. I can adjust it easily. I can move things around easily, and then once they're in there on my database and I can delete them off the excel sheet.

Six Stages of Engagement

Let's move on to the six stages of engagement. Now this is a process that I have developed and use in my dance school that really clarifies bringing those customers back to you and actually turning up to the class.

Stage 1 - The email/call/text/Facebook inquiry from the parent about a class.

Stage 2 – Your response with an offer of a class, whether it's whichever class you may feel is suitable, or an option of two or three classes.

Stage 3 - Email back from a parent saying, yes, please. We would like to take a place on x class.

Stage 4 – Your response sending another email confirming the booking. This is the really important one that states 'I am confirming your booking, the date, the time, the venue, the cost, what they need to bring.' If you have a welcome handbook or letter, send it with this email.

The differences between booking and saying 'Oh yeah, you can just call in to that class or we can just drop into that class if we want to' are huge. It's the mind-set between calling in and booking you in.

When you say 'Just call in' you can often get 'She's not feeling too well, maybe we'll just leave it this week and we'll call in next week' or 'Something came up' and you are left wondering whether they need the space or not. Whereas, on the other hand, with a booking, you get: 'Can we change the booking to next week?' It causes action in your customer. That's the difference between drop-in and booking, so make sure that that stage for that class booking is in your process.

Stage 5 - Send an email or a text message just to confirm that booking before they arrive, so on the morning of the class or the day before, they just receive a quick text message to say, looking forward to meeting you.

Stage 6 - After the class you send an email to check in and see if they enjoyed the class. It's a follow-up.

The six stages of engagement is a really solid process that encapsulates those three Cs that I talked about at the beginning. So there is the clarity, there is the consistency and there is that call to action.

So look at ways of developing your own system, encapsulating the six stages of engagement. Customers don't just contact you for classes through email. They may call, or contact you via Facebook, Instagram, or text. Whichever form of social media you are on, they can contact you, so the process needs to work on all levels. Work out your process on the various forms of contact, and once you have this process in place, it will make your enrolment quicker, easier, and there will be a lot more take up on your trials because you have the six stages of engagement.

Work out your system of how people contact you and how you can get them into the 6 stages of engagement.

CALL	FACEBOOK	EMAIL	INSTAGRAM	TEXT
↓	↓	↓	↓	↓
? Next Step?				

Whichever form they contact you – make sure you take their email address! (with permission!)

Summary

Get clear on your process, and the pathway that your customer will follow, make it consistent and don't forget that call to action or the email!

Be strong even when you have all the reason in the world to be small. Do this, just because we need you. The world needs more people with a courageous heart.

– Brendon Burchard

Chapter 17

PREPARATION, POLITICS AND GOING COOCKOO

Preparation, politics and going cuckoo

So now we move into the section of the book where you have opened your school, you have students to teach, classes to prepare for and mums and dads to deal with. You will (if you have followed the advice) know your numbers, break-evens and you will understand which classes are the ones you need to be putting more effort into if you haven't already gained the numbers you needed on opening night.

With all the preparation in the world, the real experience doesn't come until you are there running your school. Learning to deal with the crowd around you asking the same questions, or a child tugging at your shirt while you are trying to deal with a parent, particularly around show time or exams. My advice for this is once again to prepare, plan, check and check again.

The more you can anticipate the questions, and get the information out there the less people will feel they need to ask all the time. Communication is key, and the more in advance you can be, the more your parents will appreciate it. Yes there are times when things are out of your control or you need to call a last minute rehearsal, and these are expected, but they needn't be that unexpected. If you know that it's highly likely that your babies are going to need extra rehearsals before their exam, then book rehearsals in advance. If you get to the exam and they don't need it – bonus, the likelihood is you will need it.

Therefore by thinking this through, you have:

a) booked the hall in advance so there's no need to scramble round trying to find a hall;

b) parents who are more likely to be able to move things around and actually attend if they know in advance, meaning you have a higher ratio of children arriving for your extras;

c) caused considerably less stress for all involved.

Anything that can eliminate stress is a winner. There are always things that happen that are out of your control (check out my case study below, which did actually happen to me!). But the more prepped and organised you are and the more your parents know and understand what's going on, the more you will be able to handle the things that do crop up.

Case Study

One Friday night midterm, my classes were running in a local school and leisure centre, one of my four venues. It's my largest venue and there were over 120 children dancing in one night, three halls and three teachers. My classes finished at 9pm, and by 10.45 the building was on fire. Arson was the cause and I don't think anyone quite expected the fire to spread as rapidly as it did. Thankfully, no one was hurt and I was not responsible for locking this building, it was council-run. I had a text from a local mum, telling me to get there fast. I imagined it was a small fire and that I would be able to return to classes the following week, maybe with a small change of hall. I was completely wrong; in fact the fire destroyed the school adjacent to the leisure centre, although the centre itself was luckily saved, thanks to the fire brigade, but was badly damaged by smoke and water.

The result was that my classes could have been indefinitely cancelled. A quick phone around on Monday morning resulted in another building that could accommodate, but it was 30 minutes away. That week I spoke to all parents individually and they had at least five emails from me keeping them abreast of the situation. Perhaps this was overkill, but the result was that only one child out of the 120 didn't continue and they all made the effort to travel. This was so effective partly because I was so organised, and partly because parents knew where they were and they appreciated the extremity of the situation and understood that I was doing my best.

Had I not been so organised with the business, there was no way I could have dropped everything and just concentrated on this, meaning the parents wouldn't have been so informed, and maybe they wouldn't all have had an individual phone call, which I attribute to keeping 119 students out of the original 120.

This is an extreme situation, but it did actually happen to me, which in part is why I am such a strong advocate of sticking to the rules and covering your ass! Because when the proverbial hits the fan, and there will come a time when it will, you are ready and have all your Ts crossed and Is dotted.

Don't think that it will never happen to you because it could! When I opened my dance school, I could never have anticipated a fire that almost destroyed my school overnight.

Lesson plans and management

How you run your school will be very individual, based on whichever board or association you are with, and whether you do exams or are a recreational school. Either way, you will need to prepare and plan your lessons. If you haven't got this yet, may I just point out that I am a massive advocate of planning and batching.

Batching is a form of time management where you bulk a task together, so I batch my Facebook posts and my tweets so that I am scheduled for a month in advance. Which means it runs on autopilot and I don't need to think about it.

Other things you can consider batching:

- Invoicing
- Database entries

- Scheduling blogs

Unspoken code of conduct

The Council for Dance Education and Training (CDET) do have a code of conduct for dance teachers; whether people hold to that is another thing. I always say that your school is a product of you; if you're an ethical teacher with honest values, you will project that in the way you write, portray yourself and mostly conduct your behaviour. Therefore the people you attract will on the whole be people who value what you represent.

So standing by the unspoken rules, such as not poaching other people's students, not opening up in the same building as another teacher or in the immediate vicinity, is important. Basically it's a matter of respect.

As with everything, there are people who don't play by the rules! Dance can be cutthroat and if you're in a small town, stepping on someone's toes is inevitable at some point. So here are a few sayings to keep you sane!

- Just remember there are two sides to every story.
- Don't add fuel to a fire.
- As long as you conduct yourself with professionalism you can hold your head high.

Everyone's perceptions of what you do, how you run your business, the decisions you make and how you conduct yourself are different. Perceptions are just that, perceptions. People don't hold all the facts and they don't have your upbringing, your values and your integrity. This is why I cannot stress enough that you need to nail your ideal client, because your ideal client will not be the same as the next dance school's. You must also get your house in order! Cover your ass and have all those documents in place.

Dealing with mums/dads!

Oh, this is a whole other book! Let's be frank, dance mums are not the ogres that the TV programmes have painted them to be. They are people whose primary concern is the wellbeing and happiness of their child, and that rightly comes first. As a teacher, your primary concern is also the child, so in theory you should be on the same page. Theory is great until it's put into practice! You are also dealing with a huge number of different personalities, so managing those differences is always going to be a challenge.

Where the differences develop is in the mind-set of what dance is. There is also a whole debate around the merits of being paid your worth in dance. There is a history in the arts, particularly in dance, of flagrant disregard for the skill level that dancers and teachers represent. Think of it in terms of a West End show – the dancers are the worst-paid members of the cast. As dancers we are encouraged to do things for experience or, even worse, for free – in order to gain exposure or CV credibility. Can you imagine a musician ever doing the same? Yet this attitude filters down to dance classes, and teachers/dance school owners are time and again found to end up teaching for the love of dance. An average one on one music class costs £20-£30, but the average dance one on one costs £8-£15, so enough said!

So how does understanding this background help you develop your method of dealing with your dance mums? It's simple really; if you always do things for free or just for the love of dance, people will expect it or take advantage of you. Set your worth and stand by it. You need to educate the parents that this is a business and at the end of the day and you need to earn your living from it. If you can establish this from the outset, it will make things so much easier down the line.

Some rules that will help you:

- **CLARITY** – of conviction, of vision, of communication, of boundaries.
- **COMMUNICATION** – (yes here it is again!) this is so key to smoothing out problems.
- **BE PREPARED** – Get out your information out in advance and stick to it.
- **RULES** – If you have rules in place, school rules or boundaries then do not change them for one child; it must be one rule for all. If you have a late fee rule and use it – then you have to use it for all the school, and every time you bill. People will start to learn where you can get 'lax' on your rules and they will flaunt them – this is not dance mums being awkward, this is human nature! If they think they can get away with it, they will! Think about how many times you have used your phone in the car! It's illegal and dangerous, yet a very high percentage of people still do, because they think they can get away with it!
- **MISTAKES** – If you make them, own them, apologise and learn from them.

I'll give you an example. A couple of years ago I had to call an extra rehearsal for a senior jazz number that was using a massive 32 metres of material in their routine. We needed time to play with it and develop what we could and couldn't do, so I called a rehearsal. I charged just the hall hire! (#stupid) I felt couldn't charge more because so much had gone out with the show and so on. One of my mums said to me 'I think you're bonkers not charging' it's your time and expertise after all. This mum was not financially rich, but she valued my work and spoke honestly about the fact that I should too. I am eternally grateful for her conversation and it really wasn't done in a nasty way at all. In fact my mind-set at the time was very low and she demonstrated to me that I am worth more than I give myself credit for. Since then, I have never just charged hall hire!

Dance schools are a personable business, you're not someone on the end of the phone that can charge what you like, and it's very hands on. So turning up in a top-of-the-range Land Rover with your Gucci bag is only going to put peoples backs up. They start to think 'my dance fees are paying for that!', but by the same token, you cannot be taken for a ride. So getting the balance right is crucial, because nine times out of ten, money will be at the root of any disagreement.

Balance, communication and quality are key. Get these right and on the whole you will have a fab bunch of dance mums who will be raving fans of your school and do anything they can to help you. There will always be an odd bad apple, and this will take strength – but what do you do with rotten fruit? If you leave it there, that apple will infect the whole bag!

I am not one for confrontation, and I tend to avoid it at all costs. Hence the reason I have numerous handbooks, forms and so on – I cover my ass! Then if someone questions something, I have a document I can refer back to. The key to this again falls back to communication – your parents need access to the handbooks and reminders that they're there otherwise it's a pointless exercise and yet another thing that a parent will say. 'Oh I wasn't aware of so and so...'

So, that was my long answer on dealing with dance mums, my short one answer is simply this: COMMUNICATE!

Boundaries

Now this is a lesson I have learnt and continue to struggle with and I have frequently paid for this lesson in tears!

A friend said to me once 'You've forgotten more about running a dance school than some have yet to learn,' and well, I partly disagree with that. Yes, I have experienced loads of things, and yes I have a business head. But I am far from perfect, and one of my hardest recent challenges has not been the dance school. Instead, surprisingly, it has been me!

Boundaries

I've put it in bold because **boundaries** are so important!

I made the mistake of:

- Answering Facebook queries at 10 or 11pm as I happened to be surfing the net.
- I would check my emails before bed and respond.
- My phone was on continually and by my bed.

I felt the world could not continue if I did not happen to get that message and respond straight away. Boy, was I wrong. If you respond to messages and emails at ridiculous times, people will think that it's OK to contact you at any time. When I first started the school 8.30pm was switch-off time; if people wanted a response they needed to wait until a regular working hour.

Today I received a message at 6.24am. I didn't respond until after school drop-off. There has to be boundaries and times when you switch off, or your business will take over your life.

Better boundaries...

- These days I don't go on Facebook later than 8.30pm. If I'm teaching till late then I look at it the next day, or Monday if it's a weekend.
- I only check my emails in work time.
- My phone is downstairs, away from me and switched off.

These changes are hard for me, particularly the sneaky wondering 'oh what if there is a problem?' Well, let's take a step back. We're not heart surgeons, and people's lives do not depend on us. Therefore, any 'problem' can wait till a reasonable hour. Don't make my mistake – set your boundaries and stick to them! It doesn't help you or the business to have blurred boundaries. And to prove my point, when I did start my school, and I did turn off at 8.30pm regardless, my school grew from 22 to 360 pupils in four years. So, quite frankly, the bulls**t excuse of my parents needing me is rubbish!

More boundaries!

When that first child leaves

When that first child leaves your new dance school, it's heart breaking and soul-destroying; thoughts come into your mind of 'what have I done wrong?' and 'Why has she gone?' and 'Is there something I could have done better?' The truth is that even if you ask why they leave (and by the way, that is feedback and it's good practise to ask so that you can improve things), they do not always tell the truth because that might mean potentially hurting your feelings, and most people don't want to do that.

However, if you say 'I welcome feedback and I'm open to it,' people are more likely to feel they can tell you the things that are going wrong. It is not always you. Sometimes they just want to move on, or swimming lessons have changed or their friend stopped, or they want to try something else. There are a whole plethora of reasons why they would leave. The key is not to take it to heart, and if the reason does lie with you and your business, now you know, so you can make any changes so that other people do not leave for the same reason.

Summary

There are things that will always drive you potty! Any business can often be a rollercoaster – we aim for an escalator but that won't always happen. Remember to set your boundaries; they will protect you from burn out! Communication is huge element of running a dance school, so work hard on that.

Before you diagnose yourself with depression or low self-esteem, first make sure you are not in fact, just surrounded by assholes.

– William Gibson

Chapter 18

COMPETITIONS, SHOWS AND EXAMS

Competitions, shows and exams

Once your dance school has been running for a while, there will come a time when you will be ready to add in a performance or an exam or start a competition team. Each of these are a massive topic and won't be dealt with in detail because this is a book about starting a dance school, and realistically none of these things are going to happen until your dance school has been running for at least a year. But it's good to summarise.

Starting a competition team

The first question you have to ask is, is it for you? The competition world is hard from a mind-set standpoint, but also from a time and commitment point of view. It involves extra rehearsals, weekend travelling and often staying away, lots of extra hour's organisation, collecting entry fees and so on. From experience there are only a couple of companies running competitions that really have the organisation spot on. Which means that you also need to deal with last minute info and changes, which could have a knock-on effect on your teams.

And you need to factor in dance mums. Oh, dance mums. As much as I praised them earlier, when you start to factor in solos, duos, medals and trophies, it gets a lot more difficult to manage this element. Basically, you have to tell them as it is and don't take any nonsense!

Rules, ages and guidelines will change with every competition, as each competition has its own rules. So for one competition, your time limit could be three minutes and for another six minutes etc. One minute your duo is dancing with eight-year-olds, the next it's with 13-year-olds! Read the rules carefully, see what's involved, completely understand what you are getting into and consult your dance mums! Ultimately they have to ferry the kids back and forth, spending their time and their petrol money and any expenses.

Attending competitions and events can be fantastic confidence builders and amazing experiences for the students, but from a dance school owner's perspective it can be an awful lot of hard work and stress. So try in advance to be ready, prepared and not to be the one who makes the mistakes on the day. That way if the competition/event isn't going well, you can do your best to lighten/ help the situation, you can't put the blame on the event company if you make the mistakes!

Exams

If your school falls under a governing body such as ISTD or RAD, then you are going to be exam-based. Only you will know when you're ready to hold exams, but there are a few things you can do to help the organisation of this in advance and as we are towards the end of this book, these will not be new!

- **Preparation** – Plan your extras in advance, as soon as you can give the dates of your exam. Give a running order of the day and then add on 15 minutes! We all know how tight and strict the exam schedules are, and therefore if you need them to be there at 1.00 put down 12.45. Stress that this schedule will run to time, and that anyone late may not be able to do the exam. Maybe you could even create your own exam handbook.

If they are new, why not sell them an exam merchandise package, so that you know they all have the correct items.

Or on the day, book a hairdresser and offer this service at a cost to the parents. Alternatively have a trial day, where the parents practise the hair and makeup in advance. Again it's about educating your parents; they don't know your expectations unless you tell them.

Run a trial exam for the children, because they will be nervous and the more you can prepare them to deal with their nerves, the better.

Be organised with your paperwork, double and triple check your entries.

Shows

This in itself is a course as there are so many facets to it. I launched the show planner in www.thedanceden.co.uk to help dance school owners get organised; but for now let's focus on the basics for a moment. It has really taken me 17 years to get to the point where I feel I can run a stress-free show! With more than 300 children, a story concept and three sell out shows – to this day the show has been the biggest recruitment drive for my school. Put on a good show, not only from the eyes of those watching, but more importantly from the children and parents who are backstage, and you will not only have a massive retention rate, but it will also be a massive recruitment drive.

Start with your running order first, before you actually create the show or even the concept, you will have children in multiple dances and multiple costume changes! There is no point getting together this amazing idea, that runs fabulously and then finding out three weeks before that Joe Bloggs will never make that change! Here are a few tips:

Concept

- **Themes** – Movies, Weather, History
- **Story** – Alice in Wonderland etc...
- **Generic** – Non-themed dance
- **Created** – A show created from a single thought or emotion

The basis of all these shows is the same – dance on, dance off. But the story and theme ones often take more work, in the sense that they need to be connected, so there might have to be some acting or linking scenes so that the audience can understand the story.

In the beginning, it's probably easier to stick to something easy. Keep checking back to the dance den, I will do a course on this, as the creation and delivery of shows is something I am exceptionally passionate about.

This is a very basic overview of the show but my five top tips to a successful show are:

1. Preparation
2. Budgeting and revisiting that budget
3. Communication to parents
4. Deadlines in place early for payments and sizes
5. Schedule

Preparation

Months in advance I request chaperones. Marketing is all done three months in advance and poster design and so on is done three or four months in advance.

The key to a show is thinking it's a project on its own, and dealing with it like a project manager. The more you can do in advance the better, because no matter how many letters/emails you send, you will always get the question - 'so, what do I need to get?'

Schedule in advance

If you know your juniors always need extras, don't leave it till the last minute. Think in advance and schedule it in.

Schedule meetings with chaperones in advance of the rehearsals so that they understand their job. That way you will field questions away from you. Schedule your technician and teachers meeting. Communication is key, and the more they understand what's going on in your brain the better. That way, they are better equipped to help you.

Budgets

Do your maths! You need to know how many tickets you need to sell to break even and where you need to cut costs if need be. Gather all your costs and figure out how much you need to charge for extra rehearsals, allow for some not doing the show.This way you give yourself some leeway.

Costumes

Oh my days, where do I start? There are a number of costume dance sites and wholesale sites that you can go to. Please be careful if buying from abroad, as you will get import duty placed on the goods as well. Do your budget; remember to add on for unseen costs – such as postage or any returns. There is no easy answer to this. This part of your show will take work and involve some stress.

Summary

The more in advance you can be with your planning, getting your staff on board, booking props, technicians, lighting, marketing – the easier it will be. Ideally we don't want to be running around like headless chickens just before the show. We want to be savvy swans gliding across the lake! The more prepared you are, the easier it is for you to deal with when things go wrong – which they always do; a costume doesn't show, the props break, the dance isn't working, the lighting is wrong. If everything is else is ready and prepared then you are more able to deal with the issues that come up. So get your planners and start prepping!

Strength does not come from winning. Your struggles develop your strengths. When you go through hardships and decide not to surrender, that is strength.

– Mahatma Gandhi

Chapter 19

COMMON MISTAKES

Common Mistakes

Here are a couple of the common mistakes that dance school owners could fall into, be aware of them and try to not let them happen to you.

1. Not thinking things through

What I mean by that is there must've been a time where you've gone in a mad panic because you have forgotten something. Or what happens if a child gets lost? God forbid – it is our worst nightmare, but what happens if that happens? Have you thought that through? Have you got things in place to make sure that never happens? Have you got a plan of action for competitions or shows or exams or open days? Have you actually sat down and thought, if I was a customer turning up, what would I get? It could be dress rehearsals that don't run to plan just because you haven't thought things through, or didn't anticipate the time, or didn't anticipate numbers of people. It could be any element.

So the solution to not thinking it through is to just stop and walk these things through in your head. Close your eyes and think the worst! Because extremes happen – I mean, the building I used once burnt down overnight! What do you do? I hope these things never happen to you, I really, really do. But sometimes they just do, you know, life's a bit of a bugger and it just throws these things at you.

I am a massive planner, so this is a big thing for me, but honestly I cannot stress how many problems planning in advance is going to solve for you later on down the line, because you've gotten everything that you need, or you've prepped weeks in advance With planning, you're not trying to fight fire and time continually. It means you're on top of it instead of chasing it. Do extra training with staff, and put in certain procedures, so that way, when things go into a mad panic or the what ifs arise, hopefully problems will be eliminated because you've put the correct procedures in place.

2. Not updating your website

When was the last time you looked at your website, your timetables, your photos, your testimonials, your links and your terms and conditions? When was the last time that you checked them all? These days, everything is moving online and if your details are not up to date you could be missing out . Even on online sites like Yell and Mumsnet, and all the different sites that are out there, such as the database sites, where people can find classes for their little ones. If they are not all up date, then you're making it hard for people to do business with you.

Go through every page on your site. Are the links working? What does the customer see when they click on things? Can you add to the news and events section? Schedule some time every couple of months to check your website and online marketing sites, and then work your way through them bit by bit.

3. Responding to notifications

Would you like to gain extra time each day? Then turn off your notifications!

When someone sends you a Facebook message, does it beep? When someone sends email, does it bleep too? One of the biggest common mistakes that dance school owners make (and I have to add many other business people too!) is to leave all your programmes on in the background blinking and beeping at you. And then human nature will go, Ooh, let me just check and see if that's important.

So you stop doing what you are doing and nip off to Facebook. The likelihood of you being side-lined once you get onto Facebook or pop back to emails is very, very high. You go, 'Well I'll just respond to this quickly, and then I'll go back to what I'm doing.' So in the time that it's taken for you to 'just nip back,' yes, that time, although you think it's only a couple of minutes, in the course of a day that time will cost you hours and hours of work. 'Just nipping back' to check the notifications on Facebook could be ten minutes. Just flipping back to do that email will be ten minutes, but what you're not taking into account is the time it takes for your brain to re-engage with what you were doing before, or you need to re-read a section and get your thought process back in line. There are statistics out there that have calculated this and it's scary! Multi-tasking is not good!

Turn off your notifications and sounds now. Allocate some time in the morning to check them, and then turn the notifications off. In the afternoon, or just before you go to teach, check again..

4. Mind-set

This is a biggie, guys.

'I'm not good enough.'

I see it so often, unfortunately, and I think it's the dancer in us. We are perfectionists, and we were trained to make each movement perfect, but at the end of the day we're also human and we're allowed to make mistakes.

There are massive highs and lows in running a dance school, and unfortunately we need to learn to ride these a little bit, like a roller coaster, and try to not let them affect you. That's easier said than done, right? As someone who has the anxiety t-shirt thanks to my breakdown, I am so passionate about helping dance school owners so they can deal with the mind-set. We come from a place of passion and when we are so close and so invested in that when it goes wrong, or someone is nasty, or leaves, we take it personally. It's really hard to say and it's even harder to do, but you've got to try and not let the downs of running a dance school really get to you.

Things that help me:

- I wake up every morning and I'm thankful I don't know who to what for, but I'm thankful.
- Always strive to be better than you were before. If something goes wrong, then learn from it. Don't beat yourself up about it. Admit it and go, you know, well that went wrong, fine, OK, but I'm human and I'm allowed to make mistakes and that's fine. And then move on and just say right. What went wrong? What do I need to do to make sure it doesn't happen again?

  You're doing this business for a reason because you have the passion and because you have the skills. So believe in yourself without sounding like a cat poster or something from *The Lego Movie*, please believe in yourself.
- Sometimes you are going to be scared, and that's OK, but if you stay scared and stay in the same place, you are never going to go forward. You are never going to achieve your goals and you're never going to grow, and not fulfilling your ambition and your dreams is worse than being scared because you can't live a life of regret. So be scared, but hell, do it anyway. Strive, go forward. What's the worst that can happen? You can fail. Well, you'll never fail. You only learn.
- There is a tendency as humans to always remember the negative and not positive. So I want you to do this, purchase a small notebook or a large one. And in this notebook start to write down all the nice things that people say about you, the moments of achievements, the parents saying how grateful they are and how you're changing people's lives. In those moments of feeling low read it.

5. Doing everything

One of the common mistakes that dance school owners make is to do everything yourself so you are single handily saving the world. Well, the avengers have got a team and they can't manage without the team and neither can businesspeople. I love this quote from Oliver Emberton: 'You can do anything if you stop trying to do everything.'

As you build your business, it is likely at the beginning you will do most things. But as it grows, you have to delegate. You have to; you've got no choice because you physically and mentally cannot do everything.

If you hate book-keeping and it takes you five hours a week to do, assuming that you pay yourself £10 an hour for admin work, then the book keeping would cost you £50. But you hate it and procrastinate over it so it ends up taking seven hours, that's a cost of £70.

Hire a book keeper. This is their job – yours is teaching dance, and they can't teach dance, so why do you think you are an expert book keeper? As a business owner we need to wear many hats, but there are some that you just need to give to the person who is trained to do it! The book keeper costs £15 an hour and takes just two hours to do what takes you seven! It costs you £30 but saves you £40 and gains you back seven hours – a full day of your time. Just imagine what you could do!

Summary

This was one of my favourite chapters to write. We are led by passion and often these little mistakes happen because we are so invested in the business. So, please re-read this chapter! If you can stop these, then you are on track to a fantastic dance school.

"Success is not final; failure is not fatal: It is the courage to continue that counts."

Winston S. Churchill

Chapter 20

CONVERSATIONS WITH DANCE SCHOOL OWNERS

Conversations with Dance School Owners

Peter Coenen - The Dance Mill

Is there such a thing as work-life balance when it comes to dance and business?

Yeah, there is. And I mean, that means it's important that you've got people around you that you can trust. But I have recently, over the last year, made sure that I'm not in the building constantly. Because I open up every morning at half past seven, because college students are here for eight o'clock, so that's every morning, Monday to Friday. Then I used to teach Zumba six times a week, so more or less every night, so that's now down to twice a week. Wednesday night is date night. I have now modified everything because I was working too many hours. I only teach Contemporary as part of the Dance Mill Academy, so that is only at Thursday 4:30, so it's not a late one. But because I start so early, even on the nights I do Zumba I'm still finishing at half past seven. So it's still a 12 and a half hour day, which is long enough.

I've made a concerted decision to stay, 'Right that's it. I'm not going to be working every single day, all the time,' and I trust in my staff to be here to lock up, to make sure everything's correct.

How did you get into further education? How did you get accredited? Did you have to train? How did you get into running all of these courses?

Well I ran a course for the local college, Halifax College, the BTEC course, before I opened the Dance Mill. And that was one of the reasons I opened the Dance Mill. So I ran that for about four or five years and that was very, very successful. Because what we did is, we didn't just run the BTEC course, but we added in technique classes as well. I've got kids that trained there at the West End, they're working in troupes, and they're all over the world, so it really did work. When we wanted to start it here, to actually get accredited myself is very complicated and very long-winded, so I went to the school, which is opposite us, and their sixth form, and said we would like to run BTEC, will you register the kids, and you pay us and we'll run it.

And I thought, 'It's a long shot.'

So basically we're linked with a school, which is called Trinity Academy. And their sixth form ... we are part of their sixth form. We deliver it in totality, they draw down the money from the government, and they pay us a percentage of it for delivering it. And that's it really. So I don't have the issues with having to deal with registering them or anything like that. They register them and we just run it. And I do know another colleague, a friend of mine. She started doing the same thing in the Bradford area, so that is one way of getting into it. Ultimately, I would like just to be standalone. In the meantime, we can go down this avenue and then just see where it takes us.

How have you got any top tips for them on how teachers can help themselves with human resources, hiring staff or some help? Or maybe they've already got a few but they're struggling with the self-employed, contract-based element where they can just call in sick. And they're maybe not as invested in your dance school as you want them to be.

You just need to be really up with legislation and make your decisions on how you're going to deal with sickness. My wife, she works for a large organization and basically they don't pay the first three days. They've got them on statutory. And that makes a difference, because if they know they're not going to get paid for that day, they're not just going to phone up and say, 'I've had a rough night, I'm not coming in.' Just do take advice. Try and get HR advice. I did a course, an online course on it. It's constantly changing and you have to keep up with it. But we've got the internet, it's all there you can find these things out. You can literally Google the question and come back with the answers. And nine times out of ten it will be gov.uk that will have the answers. So I mean I do my own wages, SAGE software, that's easy to do. And I have a great accountant, who comes and does all the BACS and that sort of thing.

What do you find the most difficult thing to source for your business? Do you find it hard for stuff for the actual building itself? Do you find it hard to find supplies? Costumes?

I don't anymore. I don't tend to. Because of all the years I've been doing it now. I used to go to the local cash and carry and get all the stuff for the tuck shop, but then I found a company who will actually, literally deliver it to my doorstep. And bring it up to the floor and everything. So that was one of the most difficult things, because I had to go and do that myself, nobody else was going to do it.

Do you have a top tip on marketing?

I'm always running promotions to get more customers. Because if the space is being used, you have kids in that space if you've got the teachers to do it, then there's more profit. So at the moment we're doing a trial, a four week trial. And I'm doing a half-price trial and I've just put winter on it, so I can run it as long as I want. You know, it will still be cold in May so I can run it as long as I like.

So no, I think, you just try things and if they don't work then move them or tweak them. I think, don't just sit there and expect everybody to come to your doorstep. You've got to be out there, you've got to be seen to be out there. We do a lot with the ... I mean I've got my Dance Mill hoodie on, but all the kids, when they're out and about and wearing them, it's advertising. So nobody's going to find you unless you go out there and put yourself out there.

You have four very big plates running at the same. What is your top tip for how you jump from one plate to the next? How do you keep them all going?

I just do. When the college is in, then during the day I can prioritize on that, make sure everything is going with that. When we've got a show coming up, that's when I kick in because I produce it, I do all of the costumes, I source all of them. eBay is an amazing place. When my teacher goes to me, 'I want 65 red leggings for ages two to three.' I'll go right over to eBay and there they are. So yeah, just it's a difficult one to say really. I just seem to do them as it comes along, as it comes onto my desk and needs doing. If something needs ordering I do it there and then. I don't put it to one side. I tend to do it when it is fresh in my mind and get it out the way, and then move onto the next thing.

I also run two businesses, so for me as well it's about prioritizing. And I have my list and then I go, 'Right, what needs to be done? What if I don't do this now is going to have a knock on effect?' Like for example, the leggings. If you don't order the leggings now and they don't arrive in time, then they're not going to be there for the show. So it's about planning, I think. I'm a big planner. So it's about planning ahead and then it's about prioritizing so that you don't let one slip.

What's the hardest thing about what you do? What's the thing that makes you just go, 'Ugh. I can't do it like this. I can't stand this?' Or don't you do it anymore?

Not anymore.

I worked hard to get to that point. No, the thing is, people say to me, 'What do you do?' I say,' I'm very, very lucky. I'm in the dance school.' It's how I earn my living now. And I get to teach kids, and my biggest thrill is when I get to teach. I actually love it. And if it's something that I don't like, I either don't do it, or I find another way of doing things. Go around it in a different way. And as we do shows and we learn how to do things differently, even though we've done that many shows I'm still tweaking the way we do it. Tweaking how to arrange the chaperones, how you make sure the kids are there on time. How you manage it when you're in the theatre. I trust the lighting technicians more than I did when I first started. I'd give them like 30 cues for one piece. He's going, 'Are you serious?' And now I say, 'What do you think? Yeah, that looks fantastic.' You've got to prioritize and make sure ... Don't over complicate things. Because at the end of the day, if those kids are on stage and they're seen and they all look lovely in their costumes, then the parents are happy. And we can sometimes over-analyse things and we can try and make them too complicated.

What's the one thing you feel most proud of about this incredible business that you have built up there in Halifax?

Kids on stage professionally. Seeing kids that I've trained ... We've just had a lovely story of one girl. She's on the BTEC and she said to me ... 'What's your dream job?' She said, 'I want to work at Disney.' So I saw an audition come up in London only a month ago, so I prepped her for it. We studied everything. I know quite a few girls that have worked there. And she got the job. And she started there two weeks ago. And she's only 18. She's come straight out of the BTEC, straight into work at Disney. She sending me messages all the time, she's so happy. I've got other kids – I went to see *Dream Girls* recently in London and one of my boys that I trained, he was on stage. That is by far is the best thing to see them working professionally.

Peter Coenen is the creative director and owner of The Dance Mill.

Natalie Perkins – Bella Ballerina

What things do you do in the USA that is good practise that we could convert here to the UK?

In terms of studio ownership, US owners think of their studios as a business, whereas in the UK it's seen as a studio first, an education centre first. My viewpoint is more that if you're not making money from your studio, your studio will cease to exist. So unless you think of it as a business first you won't have anywhere to grow from, so you really have to start there even if your passion is what's leading you and not your ability to make money.

How do you balance home and dance school life?

When people ask me that I usually say there is no such thing! Sometimes you have to recognise that there will be days or weeks or months where your studio comes first. And you're going to spend way more time on your studio than you are on family, and that's ok. Your family has to understand that during those times when you're at your studio, they shouldn't call unless somebody's bleeding or your house is on fire. On the flip side, there's going to be ebbs and flows in the other direction and there are going to be times where your family comes first. You're going to have holidays you just want to spend with your family and not worry about the studio, there's going to be vacations where you don't want teachers from your studio calling you. So to have everything set in a way where you're not 100% tied to either, to your detriment to the other, it makes a lot of sense. There's going to be times where one takes precedent but that's OK, and you have to live unapologetically for that.

Best tip for dealing with dance mums?

This is a bit tricky for us as our dance mums have really little kids, so we don't encounter the competition mums, the super-serious dance mums. But I will say we do encounter the dance mums that have something to say about everything. The one thing I would say to a studio owner is know who you are, know what your studio stands for. You can't really apologise for it, but you have to listen to everybody. I used to hate listening to parents who would complain about little things and I just thought, get over it, it's not your choice! But, once you stop taking offence to it and just start listening to what their saying, there are some really good nuggets. I took it as a challenge; I generally say, develop your policies on the rule and not the exception. If 99 people are happy and 1 is upset, we're not changing the rule. But that one person that's upset, I am going to listen to them, because if maybe there's something in there that I can change to make them happy, it would make the other 99 a hundred times happier. It's still really important to listen with an open ear. I always tell our parents that are complaining 'Thank you.' I like to hear the good, bad and ugly because otherwise I don't know how to change my studio for the better.

What words would you say to your younger self?

I would say, go for it sooner! I waited and waited and went through so many different business ideas before finally feeling confident enough to take the leap. I don't know what I was waiting for. The longer you go in life to take chances, your personal life is going to progress too, which means as you age you might get married and have kids and more is at stake. Or you're in your current job and you're going to earn more and more and it gets harder to justify leaving that to do your own thing. There is no reason you should be waiting for anything, if you want it go do it. You don't like your life? Change it. You don't like your relations? Get out of it. Move forward; take a leap whenever you feel like it needs to be done.

What do you wish you got your head around earlier in your business?

Probably the importance of company culture and how it affects your entire staff's performance. You are the studio owner, and even if you have really great managers in place, company culture is not something you can delegate. I can show my managers what my expectations are, what we do, how we treat people and how we treat our employees, everything. But, if I don't follow up and I don't have direct conversations with the lowest people on the totem pole, then the company culture doesn't hold up and I can't just delegate it to somebody else. You are the head of that, so you have to show people what your expectations are and you do that through what you abdicate and what you don't abdicate. You have to have that consistency and it really leads to better performance. If you have a very clear vision of what your company culture to be like, then you will attract people wanting to work for you and they will perform better for you, and you'll repel people who do not agree with that. If you explain that from the interview forward you'll be hiring the right people and they will perform better for you.

What are you most proud of?

From a company perspective, the growth. How much we've been able to accomplish in a short space of time. It's been an incredible amount of work putting everything together, not just for our studio but all the studios that utilise our programming, it's an incredible amount of work and still continues to be because it's forever creating content and that is a lot of work. So I am proud of that. From a studio perspective – my favourite thing is when I hear a parent whether it's to me or to a teacher saying 'My daughter is a completely different kid, she's completely come out of her shell, she's really enjoyed her time here.' It's so much more than a dance studio, that one on one impact you have with a kid in your dance class – that is still a huge source of pride for me.

Dance schools require juggling many balls in the air at once. What's your top tip for helping cope with that?

I am a big list maker! All of our studio owners and managers have really nice planners, I like electronics, but I like paper and pen too. There are a lot of big picture items and a lot of nitty gritty detail items that we have to keep track of that are split into categories. I have major paper lists of everything divided by category and week to week basis I go to those lists and I pick a few things off them. I don't ever feel like my week to week list is super overwhelming, it's doable, I can accomplish it. But there are still these huge lists that we work off, but these are shared between the entire team and we all know what the game plan is for the future and who is working on what.

Natalie Perkins is the CEO of Belle Ballerina programme.

Conclusion

If I had known everything that I would go through when I opened my first dance school 18 years ago, I have a feeling I might have said, 'hell, no way, I'm not doing that for the next 20 years!' But we can't see the future, and although I've been through loads of ups and downs, I wouldn't ever change my decision to start a dance school. You go through periods of teaching when you feel lethargic or uninspired, when even getting to the studio feels like a drain. Then all of a sudden, something cheers you up, a nice message from an appreciative parent, a song that inspires you, a little one laughing her socks off! And within seconds you bounce back and you love teaching all over again.

The strains of running a school, particularly the time limitations and the added pressures of a show, can drag you down. When you get stupid question number 786 from parents who just haven't read the letter, and you feel like you want to scream, it's easy to walk into class carrying the stress with you, the weight of the unfinished To Do list, or the jobs that just got pushed to the side (usually marketing – now that has got to change!)

But the flipside of this is that running your own school, being your own boss, is the most amazing thing in the world. When I think back to all those children who walk that little bit taller or the mums almost in tears as they say how dance has transformed their child's confidence, regardless of budgets, money, marketing and the million other jobs you need to do as a dance school owner, those moments are the reason WHY we do what we do.

You have a gift, so now is the time to step forward and make a difference.

...

The Dance Den website is dedicated to helping dance school owners with the business of dance. A site like this can offer support and advice whilst you gain valuable business coaching on marketing, gaining more students, income streams. So become part of the 'den' and join likeminded dance school owners. www.thedanceden.co.uk